HEADS YOU WIN, TAILS YOU WIN

The Inside Secrets to
Rare Coin Investing

Jeffrey J. Pritchard

HEADS YOU WIN, TAILS YOU WIN

*The Inside Secrets to
Rare Coin Investing*

RESTON PUBLISHING COMPANY, INC.
A Prentice-Hall Company
Reston, Virginia

Library of Congress Cataloging in Publication Data

Pritchard, Jeffrey Joel.
 Heads you win, tails you win.

 Bibliography: p.
  1. Coins as an investment. 2. Coins—Collectors and collecting. I. Title.
CJ81.P814   332.63   82-5388
ISBN 0-8359-2808-X   AACR2

Editorial/production supervision and
interior design by Camelia Townsend

10 9 8 7 6 5 4 3 2 1

PRINTED IN THE UNITED STATES OF AMERICA

To Amanda

CONTENTS

INTRODUCTION

Ever since the post-World War II era, rare coins have been recognized for their investment potential. In those short thirty-eight years, coins have surged in both their value and their acceptance by the investment community. A large market has grown in a field once inhabited only by hobbyists.

In the late 1940s, when inflation was less than 3 percent a year and rare coins were considered a hobby rather than an investment, Harold S. Bareford systematically began collecting gold coins. In 1978, thirty years later, 242 gold pieces for which Bareford had paid $13,832 were sold at public auction for $1.2 million—eighty-seven times his cost.

This book's purpose is to explain why this phenomenon has taken place and what has made rare coins such an attractive and viable alternative to more traditional investments. Most importantly, this book will enable you to share in the capital appreciation of rare coins while greatly reducing downside risk and avoiding common pitfalls.

There are scores of "investment" publications that promise readers villas in the French countryside or ski chalets in Switzerland. These "get-rich-quick" books seduce investors into believing wealth is easily acquired and theirs for the asking. This book will not.

This in no way belittles the investment and appreciation opportunities that exist in the rare coin field, but investing in coins takes time, a good deal of patience, and strict adherence to specific guidelines and principles. Basic concepts must be understood before any profits can be obtained, and it is these fundamental concepts to which this book addresses itself. It discusses them in concise terms and examples so you can seize the information without wading through rivers of needless information.

In the aftermath of the incredible appreciation occurring in 1974–5 and 1979–80 and the subsequent publicity, many investors jumped blindly into the rare coin market, ignorantly and unscrupulously advised. Many invested in low-grade items, numismatic oddballs, horrendously overpriced material, and even counterfeits. Rare coins are a sophisticated investment. Those that invest through ignorance will invariably lose a good deal of their capital.

I remember one client in particular. Upon explaining to her that her $3.00 gold piece was counterfeit, she burst into tears. She had paid several thousand dollars for an item worth about sixty. However I have also had clients who inherited several coins from a grandparent and found the coins to be worth a small fortune.

If the past is any indication of the future, rare coins will continue to be an excellent investment vehicle, and although rare coins may not produce overnight millions, they can make you substantial profits and increase your net worth considerably.

1

RARE COINS AS AN INVESTMENT VEHICLE

*E*very four or five years a masterpiece painting changes hands and brings a record price, such as $5 million for a da Vinci, or a Rembrandt, or perhaps a Michelangelo. Shortly thereafter a flurry of publications report the price as excessive—a price that is beyond all reason and rationale.

Five or so years later, a new record is established, and a flurry of articles again appear questioning the sanity of the purchaser. After all, why would anyone pay millions of dollars for "just a painting"?

This phenomenon is illustrated in the table below. Note that these are different paintings. If Rembrandt's "Aristotle" sold at auction today, it would easily surpass $20 million.

HIGHEST PRICES PAID AT AUCTION

1961 Rembrandt's "Aristotle Contemplating Bust of Homer"
$2,300,000

1967 Leonardo da Vinci's "Ginevra de Benci"
$5,000,000

1970 Velazquez's "Portrait of Juan de Pareja"
$5,440,000

1980 Turner's "Juliet and Her Nurse"
$6,400,000

While these prices are substantial, it is sobering to note that when the "Mona Lisa" was assessed for insurance reasons in 1961–2, it was valued at $100 million.

Throughout history, mankind has placed a high value on art, and as long as mankind is able to appreciate an object's beauty, its aesthetics, fine art will always be highly prized, even in times of war.

One of the first things Caesar took when his invading armies conquered the known world was the art of Greece: its sculptures, its tapestries, its mosaics. When Napoleon conquered Europe, one of the first things he seized was the art of those he defeated: the paintings, jewelry, sculptures, and other masterpieces. "To the victor go the spoils" was widely practiced in World War II, as the articles below report.

Life Magazine, June 11, 1945

In a requisitioned hotel at Unterstrin, a little Bavarian town near Berchtesgaden, the world's most incredible and most valuable private collection of art works was on view last week. The staggering conglomeration of famous masterpieces had been the private property of Hermann Göring. The treasure (estimated value $200,000,000) was discovered in the sealed room of an underground cave by troops of the U.S. 101st Airborne Division, who were scouring the countryside looking for caches of gold bullion.

All the facts on how Göring "bought" these treasures are not known, but juggling the state funds and intimidation proved helpful. For years Göring, who collected medals and uniforms at will, was frustrated because masterpieces which he coveted were owned by individuals or museums in other countries. When the Wehrmacht began taking over one country after another, his collection began to grow and improve. He suddenly acquired Rubens, Rembrandts, Van Dycks, Velazquezs, Bouchers, Botticellis. His collection also included statues, gilded church panels, gold and silver ornaments, exquisite china and porcelain.

Associated Press, July 22, 1945

FLORENCE, Italy—Thirteen freight carloads of art treasures estimated to be worth more than $500 million rolled into Florence today. Heavily guarded by American M.P.s they are being returned to the galleries from which they were looted by Germans to swell the collections of Hermann Göring and other Nazi "connoisseurs."

When the Allies threatened Florence the Germans dumped the pictures and other works into trucks and fled to Balzano, where they ran out of gasoline. The trucks were left to stand for two days in a public square during rain and Allied aerial bombardment. Finally the Germans moved some to San Leonardo, about 40 miles from Balzano, and others to a prison camp about 60 miles northwest of Balzano.

During inflationary periods, times of recession, depression, or entire economic collapse, there will always be individuals willing to pay great amounts, or make great sacrifices, for the art objects that are very beautiful, or very historically significant.

From an investment standpoint, rare coins most certainly can be classified as art, as can antiques, fine oriental jade carvings, and a number of other items which investment advisors smugly refer to as "collectibles." Fine art, rare coins, Persian rugs, and quality antiques are highly valued not only for their scarcity, but also for the craftsmanship involved in making the beautiful object. The more aesthetically pleasing these items become, the higher they are valued.

Categorizing rare coins as art is not limited to this writing. Most major museums display coins of earlier countries and civilizations. The Hermitage in Leningrad boasts one of the finest collections in the world. The Smithsonian Institution has an impressive collection, and there are nearly 100 museums in the United States that have coin or currency displays.

The rare coin market is still in its infancy in comparison to other art forms. At the time of this writing, the highest amount ever paid for a coin at public auction was $725,000 for the Brasher Doubloon. (The highest price ever paid for a postage stamp was $825,000.)

A common misconception held by many individuals is that the interest in rare coins represents a speculative bubble ready to burst. Coin appreciation has even been compared to "Tulipmania," an event occurring in Amsterdam in the late 1600s in which the price of tulip bulbs was bid up astronomically. However, the supply was limitless, and the market eventually collapsed.

The interest in rare coins, and coin collecting, is not a passing fad. The first coin firm, Spink & Son of London, was founded in the mid-17th century, prior to the founding of the New York Stock Exchange. Some of the more noteworthy coin collectors include Rome's Emperor Augustus, the Medici family of Florence, John Quincy Adams, Egypt's King Farouk, and even Nelson Bunker Hunt.

The coin market's roots are not only historically deep, but they also maintain great breadth in the present. It is estimated that there are over 8 million coin collectors in the United States today.

Most importantly, art and rare coins, unlike more traditional investments, have a very limited supply. There are only a certain number of Rembrandts. That's a fact. There will never be any more. Although the demand for them increases, the supply can

4

only remain static. The increasing demand creates bidding for those few that are available, and thus the price increases. Investment grade coins, just as paintings by the great masters, appreciate because of a severely limited supply.

The beauty, craftsmanship, and characteristics of investment grade coins can never be duplicated. They are unique and irreplaceable. This fixed supply, combined with the increasing demand, creates a superb investment during inflationary periods.

WHAT IS A RARE COIN?

Rare coins are not Krugerrands. Rare coins are not bags of pre-1965 U.S. silver coinage. Rare coins are those coins that have a numismatic value higher than the metal they contain. They are coins that were minted in low quantities and of which few specimens have survived.

No antique collector would spend $250,000 for a Chippendale chest of drawers for its wood or spend $55,000 on a Louis XV snuffbox to obtain its silver. Antique collectors and investors buy such items because few were made and even fewer have survived. As a result, both the chest of drawers and the snuffbox are highly prized. So it is with rare coins.

Recent proof sets (coins specially minted for collectors) and mint sets do not qualify under this definition because millions are produced, and those same millions will probably be in existence twenty to thirty years from now due to the number of coin collectors in the country. The table below illustrates the incredible number of proof sets made each year.

RECENT PROOF SETS

Date	Mintage
1976	4,149,730
1976 (3 piece)	3,295,714
1977	3,251,152
1978	3,127,781
1979	3,677,175
1980	3,547,030

Recent proof sets are worth more than the metal they're comprised of but so many are minted that they fail to meet the criterion of rarity. Compare the recent figures with proof mintages of silver coinage from an earlier era.

5

EARLIER PROOF PRODUCTION

Date	Mintage
1906	675
1907	575
1908	545
1909	650

The market is so flooded with recent proof sets that they will never substantially appreciate. It would take incredible circumstances for the current sets to become rare.

An excellent example of this is the 1968-S proof sets, which were heavily promoted because they were the first proof sets minted in San Francisco. Sold by the government at $5 each, the sets climbed to $16 within six months. However, the $16 buyers were purchasing 25, 50, or 100 sets at a time. This was speculative demand as opposed to collector demand. The bubble burst with the sets falling to $7 in less than a year, followed by a slow attrition to $3.75. In 1981, thirteen years after their issuance, the sets were listed at $4.75 bid, and $5.15 ask.

However, in earlier years, as the table above shows, so few proof sets were produced that even if all survived today, they would bring a significant price in the marketplace.

Rarity, however, must be balanced by collector demand if coins are to be utilized as an investment. Coin collectors are the foundation of the rare coin market—they support it. Since value is a function of supply and demand, even if a specific coin is unique, it is worthless if no collectors desire to have it.

1866 Two Cent Piece. This small denomination was the first U.S. coin to carry the motto 'In God We Trust.' Courtesy Paramount Rare Coin Company.

Patterns are an excellent case in point. Patterns are trial pieces the mint creates to test possible designs for future coinage. Most patterns are made in very small quantities, yet they have lagged far behind regular U.S. coinage in rates of appreciation. An acquaintance of mine purchased a pattern for approximately $2,500. Although there were only a dozen or so known to exist, four years later when he resold it he made only $200 on the transaction.

Most collectors consider patterns a "step-child" of numismatics, and as a result, despite technical rarity, there is a very limited demand for these items. (There are a smaller number of investors per coin.) This aspect of demand will be discussed in greater length further in this book, but for now bear in mind this imperative fundamental: A coin must be rare *and* be sought by a significant number of collectors if it is to experience the appreciation investors are seeking.

This then is the definition of a rare coin of investment value: a combination of rarity and collector/investor demand.

DO COINS FIT YOUR PORTFOLIO?

Rare coins, just as any other investment vehicle, have specific characteristics that differentiate them from other investments. These characteristics determine whether rare coins are appropriate for your investment portfolio. Just as tax-free municipal bonds are not right for everyone, rare coins are not suited to every investor. Their suitability is determined by the interrelationship between the characteristics of rare coins and a variety of personal, investor considerations.

Characteristics of Rare Coin Investments

Confidentiality One characteristic that in my own experience as a coin dealer has proven itself a key factor influencing many investors is the aspect of confidentiality. Unlike stocks, bonds, or money market funds, rare coins are entirely unregulated by government agencies. As such, coins can be bought and sold in complete confidentiality. An individual can amass a substantial portfolio without the government, relatives, or even the investor's spouse knowing about it. By purchasing coins for cash, no one ever need record your name, not even the coin company making the sale. An investor can remain completely anonymous.

7

The Morgan Silver Dollar is one of the most popular coins due to its beauty and affordability. Courtesy Bowers and Ruddy Galleries.

Liquidity   Rare coins possess the most advanced market for any of the collectibles. There are an estimated 3000 coin dealers in the United States serving approximately 8,000,000 collectors. There are two dozen major numismatic auction houses in the country, a national teletype service connecting over 600 dealers, weekly publications reporting coin prices, and over fifty newsletters providing in-depth analysis of specific coins and market trends.

This combination of communication innovation and the sheer size of the collecting/investing population provides better liquidity than exists for any other collectible.

Simplicity   Once the proper coins have been purchased, timing is not a critical factor as it is for more volatile investments. Although there are peaks and valleys in the rare coin market, the long-term trend is upward, providing excellent returns for the investor who buys and holds over the long haul. This fact eliminates complicated administration and management decisions, paperwork, and fees.

Long-Term   An investment in rare coins is similar to an investment in undeveloped land (without the property taxes). The most important attribute for the investor to possess is patience. In both cases the payout is a number of years down the road, with a quick profit the exception, not the rule.

Rare coins appreciate in cycles coinciding with the general business cycle. In periods of inflation, investment dollars are funneled toward hard assets, and during this time the greatest gains

8

are seen in rare coins. In periods in which the inflation psychology is broken and confidence in the dollar is strong, the coin market's growth slows. These cycles can last anywhere from four to ten years. A five-year minimum holding period is recommended so the investor is able to partake in the profits occurring when the market dramatically and without warning explodes, tripling in a matter of months.

In addition to the recommended holding period of the investment, rare coins pay no quarterly dividends or interest, such as money market funds do. Thus while the investor is actually developing a portfolio his or her funds are "tied-up." This could actually be a disadvantage to an investor requiring a steady income from his or her investments.

However, coins can provide a continuous cash flow once the investor has properly diversified. By purchasing an assortment of coins, an investor can sell them one at a time as capital is required. Hopefully, as portions of the portfolio are sold, the balance continues to appreciate, so that the actual capital held in the rare coin portfolio remains approximately the same.

Personal Considerations of Investors

Types of Investors   Despite the wide variety of investors, who place their funds in comic books to bonds, scotch whiskey to stocks, and race horses to rare coins, there are essentially only three classifications that most investors fit into.

1. *The conservative investor*   This individual seeks an investment that stresses safety and income. The conservative investor first aims to preserve his or her capital and, second, to earn a moderate, stable return on capital. This individual's portfolio would be heavily weighted with money market funds, bonds, certificates of deposit, insurance, savings accounts, and possibly blue-chip corporate stocks.

2. *The enterprising investor*   This person will take more risks than his or her conservative counterpart. He or she is interested in capital growth and a more generous return. The enterprising individual desires an investment to both offset inflation and exhibit real growth, approximately equal to that of the economy.

3. *The speculating investor*   This person takes the most risks. He or she will buy and sell frequently in an effort to achieve

9

the greatest capital gains in the shortest period of time. However, the speculator always faces the probability of losses on a percentage of his or her holdings. This individual is also willing to incur a great deal of debt, operating in a highly leveraged position. This investor will occasionally purchase options, futures, and speculative stock issues.

An investor's classification determines what type of investments that individual will feel comfortable with. Aside from financial security, an investment should provide peace of mind. A conservative investor who has purchased commodity futures will spend many a sleepless night worrying over minute day-to-day market fluctuations. However, a speculator would quickly become frustrated if all of his or her investments were tied up in a savings account. Matching the right investment with the personality of the investor is an important consideration so as to maintain the investor's mental well-being.

Rare coins fall into the enterprising area. Growth rates can be substantial if held for the recommended period of time. If coins appear as too conservative or too speculative, you might consider using them to better balance your portfolio, adding greater growth potential to the conservative's holdings and some stability to the speculator's.

Time of Life   Your age and the age of your family will have a profound influence upon your financial needs and concerns. There are periods of your life in which rare coins are more suitable to your financial needs than in other times. Financially speaking, there are five stages in your life.

1. *Period of time prior to marriage*   This is the period from your first paycheck to the time when family responsibilities and expenses are beginning to increase. This is the time of virtually no financial responsibilities, other than yourself, and little or no need of insurance for the protection of other people.

   An investor can make higher risk investments during this period because if losses occur he or she would have ample time to start over again. It is an excellent time to begin accumulating rare coins simply because time is on your side. Even if you can only put aside a small amount, the potential growth of capital over a long period, forty to fifty years, is substantial due to the power of compounding.

During this stage, investment planning should have long-range growth objectives, particularly since income from investments shouldn't be a major necessity while only supporting yourself.

2. *Period before children*   Today it is common for young married couples to delay having a family. With both spouses working, there is an opportunity for a substantial combined income. This creates the possibility of developing a significant net worth before the responsibilities of children come along. Often this is done by purchasing a house or condominium, but again, it is also an excellent time for rare coin investment with after-housing investment funds.

Insurance is not a major factor at this time. Since both people are working, the survivor would not have undue difficulty supporting him or herself in the event of the spouse's death.

If a young married couple keep their expenses at a moderate level, a significant amount can be available to develop an investment program. (Excluding the couple's home, which is in of itself a superb investment.) Unfortunately there is tremendous pressure to spend money in the early years of marriage—to buy nice furnishings, to travel, to have two cars, to enjoy the good life. Additionally, due to the limited time each spouse has available, there is the natural tendency to purchase a great many "convenience" items and appliances.

Careful budgeting should be developed during this period so that a couple can establish some kind of investment program.

3. *Period before children are in college*   From the time of pregnancy to the time children graduate from college, assuming they choose to do so, there are a great many financial responsibilities that must be met.

Protection of the spouse and children in the event the major wage earner should die is perhaps the most important aspect of investment planning at this time. This responsibility increases with the size of the family. Insurance needs should be carefully considered, as well as the most economical way of obtaining adequate protection.

This period is also one in which spending money may be the best way to use it. There is the need for additional cloth-

11

ing, food, and housing; and basic expenses increase significantly. There is also the need for travel and vacations, and substantial educational expenditures may be required if private schooling or special educational programs are elected.

During this time, income usually increases substantially and tax planning becomes an important issue. It is also a time after the children get into elementary schools and the spouse of the primary earner can think about doing something other than housework. This could mean supplemental income for the family, which could be invested into rare coins, or other investments.

It is at this time that the problem of financing college expenses should be considered. Additional family income invested in rare coins can be a partial solution. Many of my present clients are using rare coins for this very purpose. One couple is already investing in rare coins, earmarked for their children's educational fund, and the children are only two and four years old. No matter how educational expenses are financed, they will be significant as children approach college age.

4. *Children no longer require support* The period following the children's education is usually the time when the earning power of the family is at its peak. American Bar Association figures indicate that an attorney's highest earnings occur between the ages forty-five and forty-nine. After the earnings peak is reached, income stays relatively stable or slowly begins to decline.

Because children no longer require financial support, expenses are greatly reduced, generating significant amounts of capital for investment. Life insurance needs should be reassessed in lieu of present family income, net worth, and age. Because children are financially independent, much less insurance should be required.

Capital saved by reducing or eliminating unnecessary payments for insurance premiums can help build your retirement account more rapidly. It is during this period in which estate planning should be undertaken because one must face up to the eventuality of dying. The individual's investment strategy can still be aimed at building capital, but the investor's outlook on risk should be more conservative.

Time is no longer on the investor's side and rebuilding an estate in this period of life is all but impossible.

5. *Retirement* Although the subject of retirement will be dealt with in great detail later, it will be briefly discussed here as well. There are only three ways to pay the bills after you've retired: You can live on charity, either from relatives or the state; you can work for your money, defeating the purpose of retiring; or you can make your money work for you. The usual preference toward the latter method is the primary goal of financial planning.

Financial independence during retirement results from planning and self-discipline in the earlier periods of your life. It requires determination, an understanding of investments, and a willingness to delay some material gratification from "now" to "later"—a willingness too many lack.

During the retirement period of life, rare coins accumulated over the years can be liquidated as needed, or liquidated and placed in a high yielding money market fund to generate income while preserving capital.

Conclusion and Recommendations

Despite the significant growth potential in rare coins, it is recommended that only 10–15 percent of your net worth, not including your house, be placed in rare coins. Diversification should exist in every investment portfolio. All your eggs should never be placed in one basket, no matter how good the basket is. *Rare coins are intended as a complement to a balanced portfolio, not a replacement for one!*

The period of life you are in combined with the long-term, no-dividend characteristics of rare coin investments should enable individuals to determine if rare coins are suited to their needs, and what percentage of their assets should be placed in a relatively illiquid asset. You should have specific concrete goals when investing in coins. Whether it is a college education for your children, a comfortable retirement, or a new home, the requirement to delay material gratification in the present for financial independence in the future will be much easier when saving for a specific goal that you truly, truly desire.

1855 FIFTY DOLLAR GOLD PIECE
WASS, MOLITOR & CO.
Mint State-65
Finest Specimen Known

1855 Wass, Molitor. Courtesy Bowers and Ruddy Galleries.

In 1849, a year after the discovery of gold at Sutter's Mill, tens of thousands of persons from all over the world converged upon California in the greatest gold rush in history. During this time, coins circulating in San Francisco were a combination of United States and foreign issues. Transactions were calculated in Mexican Pesos as often as in American Dollars.

As gold discoveries increased, so did commerce and the subsequent need for coin and currency. In response to this need, many banks, assayers, and private individuals produced their own gold coinage. One such group was Wass, Molitor & Company.

During the gold rush Wass, Molitor & Co. struck five, ten, twenty, and fifty dollar gold coins. After initiating mintage in 1852, no coins were struck in 1853 or 1854. Later in 1855 they introduced twenty and fifty dollar gold coins, and despite a large number of fifty dollar pieces being made, only a handful survived in good condition.

Today most Fifty-Dollar Wass, Molitor & Co. coins are in fine to extremely fine condition. This is because these were the "workhorses" of circulating coins in their day. They were not made for presentation pieces, or to test dies, but were made to go directly into circulation, of which all but a few specimens did.

To illustrate the coin's rarity in high grade, neither *A Guide Book of United States Coins*, nor Scott's *Encyclopedia of United States Coins*, prices the coin in any grade higher than extremely fine.

As part of the incredible Garrett Collection, this specific piece last changed hands in early 1980, at which time it brought $275,000.

2

THE INVESTMENT
VALUE OF RARE COINS

> For each of the four hundred and four bodily ailments celebrated physicians have produced infallible remedies, but the malady which brings the greatest distress to mankind—to even the wisest and cleverest of us—is the plague of poverty.
>
> "The Japanese Family Storehouse," Book II, Ihara Saikaku
> 1643–1693

*F*ranz Pick called rare coins "the number one hedge against inflation."

"As a hedge, rare coins historically have offered excellent protection in periods of inflation, devaluation of currencies and serious economic recession," states Max Liebler of Sherson, Hayden, Stone.

Rare coins have proven themselves an excellent investment in years past, yet it is during inflationary periods in which coins appreciate the most rapidly.

INFLATION—A CASE FOR RARE COIN INVESTING

A little over 250 years ago, in 1719 in Paris, an amazing man by the name of John Law refined, developed, and promulgated an amazing product—paper money. There had been earlier paper notes. Marco Polo brought back notes from China, handwritten on rice paper, but 1719 was the first time paper money was issued to the public on a widespread basis.

What a miracle it was! Frenchmen no longer had to burden themselves with large amounts of silver or gold coinage. They didn't need to carry any! By the end of 1719, John Law was praised as a genius. He became French Minister of Finance and was named to the French Royal Academy of Science, a group usually reserved for the likes of Sir Isaac Newton. France had become the envy of Europe, commerce flourished, and all in France were happy.

But then something peculiar happened. John Law and the government began printing too much money. After all, here was a way to pay off the government debt, help feed the poor, and pursue other noble causes—print more money. As a result, inflation raised its head.

The presses continued rolling until there wasn't enough gold or silver in the entire kingdom to back the number of notes circulating. Shopkeepers increased prices until they could no longer keep pace, and eventually they would not accept the paper money in payment. Inflation began to snowball.

John Law tried to quiet the public's fear. To prove to Parisians that some of the old notes were being retired and destroyed he burned great baskets of the notes in front of his bank. The scheme backfired. Parisians looked on, thinking to themselves, "If the Minister of Finance himself burns the money, it must surely be worthless."

Inflation turned to hyperinflation, and the worthless notes ruined thousands who had placed their life savings in them. One man slit his throat with a straight razor while seated at a table piled high with the worthless notes. A cartoon of the period appearing in Paris' "Mirror of Folly" illustrated that John Law's money was now only good for toilet paper, and Voltaire, renowned philosopher of the period remarked, "Paper has now been restored to its intrinsic value."* Finally, in December 1720, John Law, financial genius and father of paper money, fled from France with his son, lucky to escape with his life. Thus ended man's first flirtation with paper money.

The experience of France in 1720 provided an excellent example to other governments on the dangers of paper money and inflation, but governments didn't learn the lesson.

In the mid-1770s a small struggling country called the United States supported its revolution by issuing paper continental dollars. The notes soon became worthless, and gave birth to the expression, "not worth a continental."

France, a country that had most assuredly learned the lesson of inflation in 1720, forgot its lesson just a few years later. During the French Revolution, in 1790, the new government issued assignats. This was a paper currency backed by the church lands, previously seized by the new government. All the government had to do was limit the number of assignats printed and the system would remain sound. It didn't. The French intended to issue approximately 400 million livres (forerunner of the franc). However, by 1796 there were 40 billion in circulation. From January 1795, to January 1796, the price of gold, measured in livres, increased 4,800 percent!! Again hyperinflation, and thousands were ruined.

---

*John Law, The Father of Paper Money by Robert Minton, Association Press, N.Y., 1975

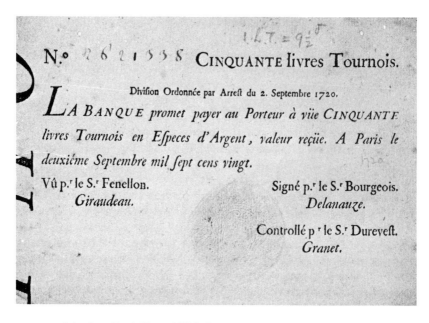

John Law Bank Note, 1720. Courtesy of Krause Publications.

Modern history has many similar examples that are more familiar: post-World War I and II in Germany, which might explain why the Mark is so stable today; post-World War II Nationalist China, when a young Chiang Kai-shek ordered printing presses run day and night to pay his army in its fight against a communist rebel named Mao Tse-tung.

Even today, there are numerous countries where inflation is over 100 percent per year, such as Argentina's 140 percent or Israel's 111 percent. Inflation has become a monetary cancer for which man has still not found a cure.

The United States has experienced periods of inflation even more pronounced than today's. The wholesale price index, measured on a five-year moving average, increased 21 percent during the Civil War, 25 percent after World War I, and 13 percent just prior to the Korean War.

From an historical viewpoint, these examples simply illustrate man's inability to control paper money over an extended period of time. The same seductive forces that caused inflation 250 years ago are present today, and modern governments are no more immune to them than their predecessors were.

In recent years, the United States has experienced double-digit inflation, and depressingly, even conservative economists feel we're headed for more of the same. In a 1981 report, the Institute of the Future gathered opinions from panels of experts and combined them with forecasting techniques to develop predictions of economic, political, and social developments. Their findings indicated an average annual rate of inflation in this country of 9 percent throughout the 1980s. Over the last 20 years, a disturbing inflationary trend has developed.

Every four to five years we have experienced periods of inflationary leaps, coinciding with the general business cycle. Most recently, these jumps occurred in 1969–70, 1973–74, and 1979–80. The discouraging aspect is that the trend is slowly creeping upward, the highs always higher than the last cycle and lows higher than the previous lows. Despite the variation from year to year, the trend is upward, as illustrated below.

INCREASE IN CONSUMER PRICE INDEX

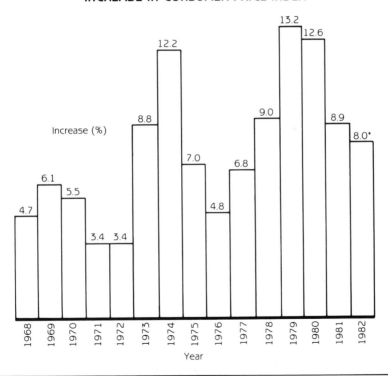

*"Official" estimates of the Reagan administration.

The problems growing out of inflation are the same as they were in France in 1720: destruction of savings, depreciation of currency, and a decrease in the standard of living.

RARE COIN INVESTMENTS COMPARED TO PAPER SECURITIES AND OTHER INVESTMENTS

This discussion of inflation is not to serve as a "chicken little" warning that our economy is on the verge of collapse. Ours is the most dynamic, divergent, and resilient economy on the planet today, but realistically, the United States faces a tough decade. The increasing money supply, rising energy prices, wages and prices chasing one another, decreasing productivity, and continued government deficit spending have created a high underlying rate of inflation that will not disappear overnight with quick government solutions. It is because of inflation, which is so deeply rooted in today's economy, that rare coins offer an attractive alternative to the traditional "paper" oriented securities and investments. The 1980s will be the decade for rare coin investment.

A study conducted by A.F. Ehrbar, appearing in the February 1976 *Fortune Magazine*, page 76, analyzed the success of paper assets as a hedge against inflation. The table below illustrates the results of the study. Ehrbar calculated what $100.00 invested in 1965 would be worth in 1975, after being discounted for inflation, utilizing the following investments:

Item	1965 Investment	Purchasing Power 1975	Amount Lost
Treasury Bills	$100.00	$99.00	$ 1.00
Savings Bank Deposits	100.00	94.00	6.00
Government Bonds	100.00	83.00	17.00
Corporate Bonds	100.00	81.00	19.00
Standard & Poors 500	100.00	81.00	19.00
Dow Jones Industrials	100.00	75.00	25.00
Lipper Growth Fund Index	100.00	63.00	37.00

None of the securities retained their 1965 purchasing power; all lost ground. Treasury bills only lost a dollar, but the Dow Jones Industrials lost 25 percent of the original investment. During the same period, investment quality rare coins doubled in purchasing power.

The growing acceptance of rare coins by the investment community is illustrated by the results of a survey made by John A. Haskett, published in Burrough's Clearing House. Haskett sought to answer the question, how do bankers invest their own personal funds? Where does "smart money" invest?

Haskett's criteria for selection of the bankers was that they had to be at least vice presidents. Three hundred officers were interviewed from New York, Philadelphia, Boston, Miami, Milwaukee, Chicago, Atlanta, Minneapolis, Dallas, Denver, Los Angeles, and Seattle.

When asked how many of these bankers invested in rare coins/stamps, twenty-five percent responded that they already did, and 52 percent indicated that they intended to do so in the near future.

These bankers also rated the negative aspects of various investments, ranging from hard assets to more traditional ones. Rare coins/stamps were ranked for security just behind life insurance, savings accounts, and certificates of deposit. Coins and stamps were ranked far superior in appreciation than the following investment vehicles:

1. Life insurance
2. Savings accounts
3. Company pension funds
4. Corporate stocks
5. Real estate (residence)
6. Certificates of deposit
7. Corporate bonds
8. Real estate mortgages
9. Mutual funds
10. Real estate (commercial)

Over the long haul, rare coins have performed remarkably well as an investment. The following table illustrates several examples. The rates of return are good, but one must realize this time period spans the 1950s, in which interest rates were 2–5 percent. In regard to the entire period of time covered, the average rates of return are phenomenal!

21

UNCIRCULATED RARE COIN GROWTH*

Coins (Unc.)	1948	1982	Annual Compound Rate of Return (%)
1853 Half-Dime (III)	$ 1.50	$ 625.00	19.4
1880 $3 Gold Piece	50.00	4,000.00	13.8
1917 Quarter (I)	2.75	250.00	14.2
1901 Quarter	4.00	425.00	14.7
1864 Two Cent Piece	1.00	225.00	17.3
1904-5 Silver Dollar	4.00	1,600.00	19.3
1884 Half Dollar	4.00	900.00	17.3
1831 Half Dollar	3.50	725.00	17.0

*Data compiled from R.S. Yeoman, *A Guide Book of United States Coins.*

Salomon Brothers of New York, one of the country's largest brokerage houses and investment bankers, traditionally evaluates a group of the most notable investment vehicles, including hard assets and paper ones. Their most recent study, published in *Investment Policy*, June 15, 1981, appears below.

SALOMON BROTHERS INVESTMENT ANALYSIS

June 15, 1981
(Compound Rates of Return)

Item	10 Years	5 Years	1 Year
Oil	30.8%	20.9%	14.3%
Gold	28.0	30.7	−13.9
Oriental Carpets	27.3	20.9	−0.2
U.S. Coins	27.1	29.7	−8.0
U.S. Stamps	23.5	32.9	18.0
Chinese Ceramics	22.9	30.7	36.5
Silver	21.5	20.1	−26.6
Rare Books	16.8	13.8	18.0
Old Masters	15.4	16.8	22.9
Farmland	14.6	14.8	9.7
Diamonds	14.5	16.9	0.0
Housing	10.3	11.6	8.1
Consumer Price Index	8.3	9.7	10.0
Stocks	5.8	9.8	25.3
Foreign Exchange	5.3	3.1	−17.3
Bonds	3.8	1.1	−9.6

The chart illustrates rare coins' remarkable long-term track record, averaging 27.1 percent annual growth for the last ten years, and 29.7 percent growth each of the last five years. The 8.0 percent dip occurring in the last twelve months is the normal "correction" stage of the rare coin cycle. This will be discussed in greater depth in the chapter on the current market.

The validity of this type of analysis, or index, rests entirely upon how the researchers have defined rare coins. What are they including or excluding? How lenient are they in their criteria of an investment quality coin? Gold is gold, and oil is oil, but many of the other categories, coins included, are too ambiguous.

Growth Rate for Rare Coins

The growth rate for rare coins in this study is good, but it can and should be better. Most indexes such as these have a fairly lenient definition of rare coins, which invariably includes lower quality items. However, by upgrading the definition of an investment quality rare coin, the appreciation level changes dramatically and places rare coins at the forefront of the hard assets above.

In a special report appearing in *Inside View*—"An Inside Report on the Rare Coin Market"—David Hall analyzes the appreciation of choice or gem quality rare coins from 1950 to 1980. These figures were gathered from R.S. Yeoman's *A Guide Book of United States Coins* and, beginning in 1971, from *The Coin Dealer Newsletter*. The findings illustrate the long-term benefits of high quality, investment grade coins.

AVERAGE ANNUAL GROWTH RATES (%)

Coin Type	1950–59	1960–69	1970–80
18th and 19th Century Coinage	16.48%	17.24%	53.17%
Gold Coins	8.51	12.75	61.09
Silver Dollars	8.90	15.51	51.91
Early 20th Century Coinage	13.17	11.53	41.00
Total Market Average:	11.76	14.26	51.79

31-year total market average growth rate: 25.9%!

Data compiled from *David Hall's Inside View, An Inside Report on the Rare Coin Market*, special report by David Hall and David Hunt, 1980.

These growth rates are virtually unmatched by any other investment, and their consistency testifies to the stability of the rare coin market. When the growth rates are translated into dollars and cents, the impact is more profound. Utilizing the "Total Market Average":

1. $1,000 invested at the beginning of 1970 into gem quality coins were worth $53,728.45 in early 1980.
2. $1,000 invested at the beginning of 1960 were worth $200,070.71 in early 1980.

3. $1,000 invested in gem quality coins in 1950 were worth $605,451.08!

Collectors/investors who have prospered the greatest are the connoisseurs who have consistently demanded the highest quality coins.

The table below illustrates the recent compound growth rate of high quality coins, all in choice condition. These are the true investment quality coins. The appreciation rates range from 50–90 percent compounded. These types were randomly selected and accurately reflect the general market for choice quality items. In addition, these growth rates take into consideration a market correction that took place during the latter half of 1980, which will be discussed later.

The reason these coins have done so well rests with supply and demand. This is illustrated in the pyramid diagrams. The pyramid on the left side represents the total market supply of rare coins. The numbers refer to the coin's condition. As the condition improves toward a flawless MS-70, the supply gets smaller and smaller.

APPRECIATION RATES OF RARE CHOICE COINS

Mint State—65

Coin Type	1-5-79	1-5-82	Compounded Growth Rate (%)
Half Cents (Classic)	$ 550	$ 2,100	56.3
Flying Eagle Cents	450	1,800	58.7
Two Cent Pieces	275	1,350	70.0
Buffalo Nickels (I)	40	225	77.8
Bust Half Dimes	600	4,250	92.0
Barber Dimes	235	1,050	64.7
Twenty Cent Pieces	1,100	5,600	72.0
S.L. Quarters (no drapery)	4,000	12,000	44.2
Standing Quarters (I-F.H.)	300	1,450	69.1
Bust Half-Dollars	975	3,700	56.0
Seated Liberty Dollars (w/m)	1,250	4,900	57.7
Trade Dollars	750	3,900	73.2
$1.00 Gold Piece (I)	850	5,000	80.5
$3.00 Gold Piece	1,850	8,000	62.9
$10.00 Liberty Gold (w/m)	425	3,000	91.8
$20 Liberty Gold (I)	3,600	10,000	40.5
$20 St. Gaudens	330	1,350	60.0

Data compiled from *The Coin Dealer Newsletter* "bid" quotations.

1856 Flying Eagle Cent. Courtesy Bowers and Ruddy Galleries.

The pyramid on the right represents demand. The coins in average condition are plentiful, and thus collector/investor demand for them is easily satisfied. However, as the coins' condition improves, demand increases. This results in more and more people bidding on fewer and fewer coins, driving the prices upward. As is shown on the pyramid, a slight increase in condition can mean a great increase in value.

SUPPLY—DEMAND PRINCIPLE OF RARE COINS
(Seated Liberty Dollars)

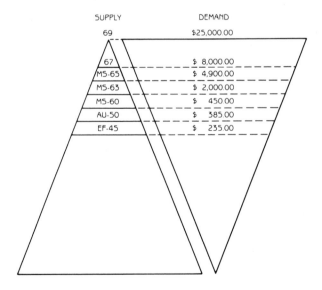

SUPPLY	DEMAND
69	$25,000.00
67	$ 8,000.00
MS-65	$ 4,900.00
MS-63	$ 2,000.00
MS-60	$ 450.00
AU-50	$ 385.00
EF-45	$ 235.00

Price levels represent a Seated Liberty Dollar with motto.

This will be explained in greater detail in the next section. However, it can be seen that the coins at the top of the pyramid are worth more today, and will be worth more tomorrow. These are the investment coins an investor must concentrate upon. Too many indexes, such as the Salomon Brothers, include the top half of the pyramid, when they should limit analysis to the top third or top fourth. That area represents the coins in which substantial profits can be made if the past is any indication of the future.

THE 1804 SILVER DOLLAR
King of American Coins
(Fifteen Known Specimens)

1804 Silver Dollar. Courtesy Bowers and Ruddy Galleries.

Silver Dollars were minted in this country from 1794–1803, but few found their way into circulation. These dollars had slightly more silver in them than the then popular Spanish Milled Dollars. As a result, large quantities of American Dollars were shipped to the West Indies and exchanged, at a slight premium, for the Spanish Milled Dollars. Spanish Dollars were then shipped back to America, exchanged at par; and the process was repeated to the profitable delight of shippers.

In 1804 President Jefferson ordered the mint to stop creating silver dollars in an effort to curb the aforementioned activity. However, before the mint received the stop order, 19,570 silver dollars were minted during calendar year 1804. However, the coins bore the dates 1802 and 1803 because in early minting practices, dies were used until they shattered.

In 1834, thirty years after Jefferson's suspension, the U.S. State Department desired to send specimen proof sets of American coinage to the King of Siam and the Sultan of Muscat. The mint director wished to include a silver dollar in the set, but production had ceased long ago.

Checking earlier records, the mint director discovered the last dollars were made in 1804, but the records failed to indicate that those dollars had been dated 1802 and 1803. The director couldn't locate a proof specimen of the 1804 dollar (because there were none) so he made new dies with the 1804 date and minted a small number of dollars. He had unknowingly created the first 1804 Silver Dollar thirty years after the coin's date.

Aside from its historical significance and notoriety, the 1804 Silver Dollar is the most valuable American silver coin. Past auction records are listed below:

1950	Dexter Specimen	$	10,000.
1960	Davis-Hale Specimen		28,000.
1961	Idler Specimen		29,000.
1970	Appleton Specimen		77,500.
1972	Idler Specimen		80,000.
1974	Appleton Specimen		150,000.
1980	Garrett Specimen		400,000.

In 1866 Mathew A. Stickney refused to part with a specimen although he was offered $1,000 for it.

3

DETERMINANTS OF INVESTMENT QUALITY COINS

\

*C*oins that have shown the greatest capital appreciation in the past are those that have been in the best condition, and those of the lowest mintage. Coins of this description, quality rare coins, show the consistent growth investors should seek. These coins have always been in demand and always will be. Quality is determined by three factors: scarcity, grading, and demand.

SCARCITY

A coin's scarcity (how unavailable it is) is the most influential determinant of its value. It's merely supply and demand. The supply of a specific coin of low mintage is less than the demand of investors or collectors wishing to own it.

There are a variety of factors that cause a coin to become rare. The most predominant is the actual mintage of the coin. This establishes the maximum number of collectible specimens of each particular year and type. (In early United States coinage, the mintage figures are not precisely known due to the irregularities of the mint's early bookkeeping procedures.) The earlier U. S. coins were not produced in such sizeable quantities as today's. This was due to more primitive minting procedures and a smaller need for currency. Compare the mintage figures below of the 1794 Silver Dollar and the first Eisenhower Dollar.

Item	Mintage	Value
1794 Dollar	1,758	$ 40,000.
1971 Dollar	127,000,000	7.

The 1913 Liberty Head Nickel has the lowest official mintage of any U. S. coin. Only five are known to exist today. These few

1794 Silver Dollar. Courtesy Paramount Rare Coin Company.

pieces were made to test the die press machinery prior to the arrival of the dies for the Buffalo Nickel. As with many other rarities, the few pieces were earmarked for destruction, but a mint employee intervened and smuggled out five of the experimental pieces.

Approximately eight years later, the same employee advertised he would pay $500 for examples of the nickel, knowing he possessed the only specimens. Doing so, he cleverly initiated demand for the 1913 Liberty Head Nickel and established a market price (after the statute of limitations had expired). The last time one of the 1913 nickels changed hands was in 1978 at a private sale; the coin brought $200,000.

1913 Liberty Head Nickel. Only five specimens in existence. Courtesy Paramount Rare Coin Company.

31

1894-S Barber Head Dime. Courtesy Bowers and Ruddy Galleries.

A similar rarity was created years earlier in 1894. In 1893 nearly 2.5 million Barber Head Dimes were minted at the San Francisco mint. In 1894 the mint prepared to strike a similar number of dimes but received no orders from Congress to do so. However, twenty-four of the dimes were struck.

One theory maintains that they were struck to balance the ledgers for that year, with an additional $2.40 necessary to round out the figures. Another theory is that the coins were made as presents for the mint director's daughter. Whatever the rationale for creating the items, they are a major rarity today with only seven specimens known to exist. Valued at $4,750 in 1958, seventeen years later at a private sale one fetched $97,000.

After coins are minted they are released into general circulation, and from that point on they begin to disappear. Coins are burnt, swallowed, made into jewelry, buried, lost, and defaced. Throughout the years coins have been intentionally melted for their bullion value. This has added to their scarcity. The United States Government is far and away the largest culprit in this regard. Two cases in point:

1. The one-dollar gold piece was first struck in 1849, and in the next forty years of its issuance, approximately 12 million of the pieces were minted. However, the government recalled and remelted 8 million of the pieces, so that only one-third have had a chance to survive.

2. A similar situation took place in 1853. The price of silver had risen to a level that made the 1853 silver coinage more valuable than its face value. Because of this, many private groups melted down large quantities of the 1853 coins for the bullion. In response, the mint reduced the silver content of coins by 7 percent. The newer coins were specifically marked so the government could withdraw and remelt the heavier coins.

A more contemporary example of destruction of silver coins happened in early 1980. Silver traded for as high as $48.80 an ounce before plummeting to its current level of $7.–$8.00. During this period untold quantities of silver coinage were removed from piggy-banks, attics, and other hiding places; sold to coin dealers; and subsequently melted to obtain the silver. Although it will be several years before the market determines the extent of coins melted and appropriately adjusts for it, this instance of meltdown will undoubtedly drive prices higher.

Invariably the question will arise: "Should I invest in a few rare coins or numerous common ones?" The answer to this is best expressed in a phrase attributed to noted numismatist, Q. David Bowers: "A common coin that is common today will be common in the forseeable future. A common coin by definition is common and not rare!"* There is an abundance of evidence to support this.

Compare two quarters minted in 1875, both in uncirculated condition. One was minted in San Francisco, and the other at Carson City. In 1963 the 1875-S was priced nearly three times that of the 1875-CC quarter; yet in the following eighteen years, the Carson City quarter surpassed the San Francisco quarter in not only rate of growth, but value as well!

GROWTH RATE COMPARISON

Item	1963	1982	Yearly Compounded Growth Rate
1875-S Quarter	$70	$ 800	13.7%
1875-CC Quarter	25	1400	23.6%

Why did the above occur? Only 140,000 of the 1875-CC quarters were minted, whereas 680,000 of the 1875-S quarters were. The Carson City Quarters were scarcer, undervalued, and more in demand than the 1875-S.

GRADING

The grading of a coin refers to how well preserved it is. As coins become older, fewer and fewer remain in uncirculated or mint state condition. They become worn as they pass from hand to hand.

---

*David Bowers, *High Profits from Rare Coin Investment*, p. 61.

The grade of a coin ranges from perfect (70) all the way down to poor (3). The American Numismatic Association has fifteen classifications for business strikes (coins made for general circulation). They are as follows:*

Perfect uncirculated (MS-70)   Perfect new condition, showing no trace of wear. The finest quality possible, with no evidence of scratches, handling, or contact with other coins. (In over ten years in the rare coin field I have only seen a few coins that could actually be graded MS-70.)

Gem uncirculated (MS-67)   This is a relatively new classification designed to fill the void between 65 and 70. This coin is decidedly better than an MS-65 but contains a tiny flaw or imperfection keeping it out of the MS-70 category.

Choice uncirculated (MS-65)   An above average uncirculated coin, which may be brilliant or lightly toned and has very few contact marks on the surface or rim.

Select uncirculated (MS-63)   On today's market the majority of uncirculated coins fall more comfortably into this category than any other. This is why the grade was created several years ago by the American Numismatic Association (ANA). There are a number of factors that place a coin in this grade rather than a higher one: weakness of strike, too many bag marks, hairlines or other man-caused impairments. If these are serious, then the coin would fall to a MS-60 classification.

Uncirculated (MS-60)   Has no trace of wear but may show a moderate number of contact marks, and the surface may be spotted or lack some luster.

Mint luster is the sheen or bloom on the surface of an uncirculated numismatic object. It results from the centrifugal flow of metal caused by striking dies. Mint luster is somewhat frosty in appearance as opposed to the mirror-like smoothness of the field of a proof coin.

Choice about uncirculated (AU-55)   Slightest evidence of light wear on only the high points of the design. Most of the mint luster remains.

About uncirculated (AU-50)   Has traces of light wear on many of the high points. All design details are very sharp. Must have at least half mint luster.

---

*R. S. Yeoman, *A Guide Book of United States Coins*, 1981, p. 4.

SMALL CENTS — LINCOLN 1909 TO DATE

EXTREMELY FINE   *Very light wear on only the highest points.*

EF-45   *Choice*
Obverse: Slight wear shows on hair above ear, on the cheek, and at the jaw.
Reverse: High points of wheat stalks are lightly worn, but each line is clearly defined.
Half of the mint luster still shows.

EF-40   *Typical*
Obverse: Wear shows on hair above ear, on the cheek, and on the jaw.
Reverse: High points of wheat stalks are worn, but each line is clearly defined.
Traces of mint luster still show.

VERY FINE   *Light to moderate even wear. All major features are sharp.*

VF-30   *Choice*
Obverse: There are small flat spots of wear on cheek and jaw. Hair still shows details. Ear and bow tie slightly worn but show clearly.
Reverse: Lines in wheat stalks are lightly worn but fully detailed.

VF-20   *Typical*
Obverse: Head shows considerable flatness. Nearly all the details still show in hair and on the face. Ear and bow tie worn but bold.
Reverse: Lines in wheat stalks are worn but plain and without weak spots.

Example of Grading Standards. Reprinted with permission of the American Numismatic Association and Western Publishing Company.

Choice extra fine (EF-45)   Light overall wear shows on the highest points. All design details are very sharp. Some mint luster is still evident.

Extra fine (EF-40)   Design is lightly worn throughout, but all features are sharp and well defined. Traces of mint luster show.

Choice very fine (VF-30)   Light even wear on the surface and highest points on the design. All lettering and major features are sharp.

Very fine (VF-20) Shows moderate wear on high points of design. All major details are clear.

Fine (F-12) Moderate to considerable even wear. Entire design is bold with overall pleasing appearance.

Very good (VG-8) Well worn with main features clear and bold although rather flat.

Good (G-4) Heavily worn with design visible but faint in areas. Many details are flat.

About good (AG-3) Very heavily worn with portions of lettering, date, and legends worn smooth. The date may be barely readable.

Damaged coins (bent, corroded, scratched, holed, nicked, stained, oxidized, or mutilated) are worth much less than those without such defects.

There is another minting procedure for coins known as "proof." Proof coins are produced for collectors. The actual minting process is different than for business strikes. In the minting of proofs, the dies (the press that bears an incuse image of the coin) are carefully made so that all features are sharp and the flat surfaces are brilliantly polished. Carefully selected planchets (blank metal discs) are fed into low-speed presses and struck several times to highlight all of the coin's features. In contrast, coins for general circulation are struck only once and at high speed.

During handling, great care is taken not to scratch or nick the proof coins. Each piece is grouped with other denominations from that same mint to form a proof set. These are then sent to collectors who ordered them. Mintage is "limited" to the number of orders.

The ANA's grading standards apply to proof coins as well.

Proof-70 A perfect proof coin with no traces of hairline scratches, handling marks, or other defects; a flawless coin. This specimen can be brilliant or have natural toning.

Proof-65 A choice proof that might show very fine hairline scratches from friction-type cleaning. To the naked eye this coin will appear virtually perfect.

Proof-60 A proof with some scattered handling marks and hair lines that are visible without magnification.

When investing in rare coins, it is advisable to buy the best grade possible. For most coins this is MS-60 or better. Utilizing the supply pyramid diagram in the preceding section, it is evident that a high grade coin (high on the pyramid) is worth substantially more than the same coin in a lower grade. More importantly, the further up on the pyramid the coin is, the faster it is likely to appreciate. Below are four randomly selected examples to illustrate this principle.

1871 TWO CENT PIECE

Condition	Year	Value	Annual Compounded Growth (%)
Uncirculated	1963	$ 30.00	15.3
	1982	450.00	
Extra Fine	1963	17.00	4.6
	1982	40.00	

1911-D EAGLE ($10.00 GOLD PIECE)

Condition	Year	Value	Annual Compounded Growth (%)
Uncirculated	1963	110.00	26.8
	1982	10,000.00	
Extra Fine	1963	70.00	10.9
	1982	500.00	

1859 FLYING EAGLE CENT

Condition	Date	Value	Annual Compounded Growth (%)
MS-65	1–79	450.00	58.7
	1–82	1,800.00	
MS-60	1–79	180.00	13.0
	1–82	260.00	

1911-D Ten Dollar Gold Piece. Mintage: 30,100. Courtesy Paramount Rare Coin Company.

1873 Seated Liberty Quarter. The arrows denote a change in the bullion composition. Courtesy Bowers and Ruddy Galleries.

SEATED LIBERTY QUARTER—1873 (w/arrows)

MS-65	1–79	950.00	
	1–82	3,800.00	58.7
MS-60	1–79	500.00	
	1–82	1,050.00	28.1

The best grading guide on the market, which sets the standards for U. S. coins, is the American Numismatic Association's grading manual. It has detailed drawings of each American coin type in each respective condition. The book also details other miscellaneous information, such as: at what points wear will first appear, if the coin was generally well struck, and if there are a great many counterfeits.

Many coins are virtually nonexistent in mint condition, due to age, extreme rarity, or a variety of other circumstances. A few such coins are

1793 Liberty Cap Large Cent

1843-O Seated Liberty Dime

1876-CC Seated Liberty Dime

1871-CC Seated Liberty Quarter

1794 Half Dollar

1870-S Silver Dollar

However, coins such as those above are excellent investments in grades such as extra fine or very fine. The essential point is to purchase a coin in the best condition possible for that specific coin.

Strike and Color—Cornerstones of Investment Grading

As price disparity increases between higher grade coins, the grading of investment quality pieces becomes critical, as well as more difficult. The difference between an MS-60 and an MS-65 is relatively slight, but the MS-65 may be worth ten times the former. This problem is intensified by the utilization of grades such as MS-63, 64, 66, 67, and even MS-68. More and more dealers utilize such grades, causing additional confusion to the collector/investor. Can there be any real significant difference between an MS-63 and an MS-64 to rationalize the price difference? Additionally, there are no books on the market to aid in the grading of coins above uncirculated (MS-60) condition. The ANA grading manual is good, but like other references, it is sketchy in regard to grades higher than MS-60.

This is due to the fact that wear is a disqualifying feature. If an item has no signs of wear, it is at least uncirculated; but to determine if it is MS-60, 63, 65, or 67, a variety of technical factors need to be addressed. The factors to consider are strike, luster, tone, and marks. Because each individual coin type is different, this is the area of grading that can take years to master and that remains somewhat arbitrary, even among the so-called experts.

Prior to discussing these factors as they relate to rare coins in general, the following discussion on Lincoln Head Pennies illustrates how these factors are incorporated for one coin type. (This piece is reprinted with permission from the October 1980, Monthly Summary, appearing *The Coin Dealer Newsletter*.)

LINCOLN CENTS

Strike The MS-65 Lincoln will be sharply struck with all obverse and reverse details strong. Coins with sharp obverse definition but with poorly defined wheatlines do not qualify, and, conversely, a mushy portrait of Lincoln coupled with sharply defined reverse details does not meet the qualifications for strict MS-65. The strike of a gem MS-67 Lincoln will be exceptional—obviously superior even to the already "choice" MS-65. It must be noted that the production standards of the three mints varied from year to year (particularly, of course, in Denver and San Francisco). The disintegration of quality was especially evident between 1917 and 1928.

1955 Double Die Lincoln Cent. Its rarity is derived from the accidental doubling of its date and lettering. Courtesy Bowers and Ruddy Company.

Therefore, some minor allowances must be made when comparing the mintmarked issues from these years to the earlier issues. Very few of these middle year coins *ever* show the sharp high relief detail of a choice or gem early D-mint. For example, if you "hold out" for a 1926-D that looks like a top quality 1915-D, you may never own one!

Marks The MS-65 example may show a few very light bag marks or some light hairlines. More severe marks—especially in "crucial areas" such as the wheatlines or Lincoln's face—reduce the coin to MS-63 or less according to the severity of the problem. The MS-67 specimen will be virtually free of any marks at all.

Color This is the most controversial area of the grading of Lincoln cents—and, indeed, it is perhaps the single most important factor. However, color is sometimes over-emphasized as almost the *only* factor affecting the grade. Far too often a full original red Lincoln is advertised as MS-65 or MS-67 even though the strike leaves a great deal to be desired. For the purposes of this article and its accompanying price ranges, MS-65 is defined as at least 90% "original red" and without detracting spots or fingerprints. (The other 10%, simply stated, should consist of attractive natural toning—not stains or splotches.)

The MS-67 coin is fully original red and, in addition, has all the other qualifications for this top category. "Original red" is not a strictly defined "color" since the coins as struck through the years were originally of varying color. Shades of gold and yellow, tan, orange and red all fall under the "original red" umbrella. In addition, some mellowing of color is natural on a coin which has been around for fifty to seventy years. An early Lincoln which is too brilliant is suspect; cleaning and recoloring have been brought to an art during recent years.

It should be added that MS-65 and MS-67 Lincolns do not all "match" and that subtlety of color which might escape the eye of many may be worth a substantial premium to others who have been seriously involved in the series for a long time. In short, grading (and pricing) by strike and marks is relatively easy once the basics are understood. When color is the factor under consideration, grading, and thus price, become far more subjective.

The in-depth analysis above illustrates the complexity of accurate grading. The following discussion explains strike and color in more general terms and shows how they apply to the rare coin market in general.

Strike "Striking" refers to the process whereby a coin receives its features at the mint. Two dies carry an incuse image of the coin's surface and strike a planchet, or slug, simultaneously, thereby creating the coin. However, as the minting proceeds, the dies striking the coins can become worn or dirty. Unless they are cleaned or corrected, they yield a coin that lacks some of the finest detail. Additionally, when worn dies are polished some of the finer details are removed.

Whereas proofs are usually sharply struck, coins minted for general circulation get progressively worse as the minting process continues. The result is that a coin can be properly graded MS-60 or MS-65, yet still be weakly struck and lack fine detail within the pattern.

An example of a weakly struck coin is the 1856 Large Cent. The left side of one of the dies was slanted, and therefore that side received less pressure in the striking process. Thus the coin's left side lacks sharp definition even on a specimen with full mint luster.

The rarity of fully struck coins is best illustrated by the development of a separate pricing structure for three coin types that are generally weakly struck. These are the Mercury Head Dime, the Standing Liberty Quarter, and the Jefferson Nickel.

The Mercury Dime's weak strike is most apparent on the reverse side of the coin. Pictured on the reverse is a fasces (representing preparedness) comprised of a battle axe surrounded by many rods bound together (representing strength in unity). At the center of the fasces are two horizontal bands. These two bands determine the fullness of the dime's strike. On fully struck specimens, two distinct bands are discernible, whereas on poorly struck coins, these two bands merge into one, or the two bands are not completely separated the entire width of the fasces. Fully struck specimens are referred to as "Full Bands."

41

"Full Band" Mercury Dime. Note that the central cross bars are fully separated. This specimen is valued at approximately $5,000. Courtesy Paramount Rare Coin Company.

This 1917-D (Type One) Standing Liberty Quarter exhibits "Full Head." Photos are twice the actual size. Courtesy C. Rhyne & Associates.

42

This Standing Liberty Quarter is approximately 80% "Full Head." Courtesy Paramount Rare Coin Company.

The Standing Liberty Quarter, due to the nature of the design, usually has a weak strike on the head and shield of Liberty. An unusually sharp strike clearly defines the tiny facial features and is called "Full Head."

The proportion of well-struck quarters varies with the date and mint. As outlined by J. H. Cline in *Liberty Standing Quarters,* this ratio differs a great deal. Whereas 25 percent of the quarters from the Philadelphia mint in 1929 are estimated to have "Full Head," only 1 percent of the quarters from the Denver mint in 1928 were fully struck.

Jefferson Nickels are a recent addition to this separate pricing structure. On the coin's reverse is pictured Monticello, Jefferson's home. On sharply struck nickels all five steps leading to the doorway are well defined. These specimens are called "Full Step" and carry a premium in the marketplace.

The added value of unusually well-struck specimens is evident in the separate pricing structure mentioned previously. Following are a few examples:

STANDING LIBERTY QUARTERS

Date	MS-65	MS-65 Full Head
1916	$6,500.00	$13,000.00
1920	740.00	2,350.00
1921	1,850.00	5,600.00
1930–S	560.00	2,100.00

MERCURY DIMES

Date	MS-65	MS-65 Full Bands
1916	$ 60.00	$ 240.00
1921	1,850.00	4,750.00
1931-D	300.00	725.00
1939-S	62.50	1,100.00

JEFFERSON NICKELS

Date	MS-65	MS-65 Full Step
1953-S	$ .50	$ 350.00
1954-S	.30	350.00
1960-D	.15	200.00
1970-D	.10	150.00

Data compiled from "*Coin Dealer Newsletter,*" January 1982.

"Full Step" Jefferson Nickel. Note the distinctive steps outside the doorway of Monticello. Courtesy Paramount Rare Coin Company.

As was the case in the grading explanation of the Lincoln Cent, if a coin is to maintain a grade of MS-65 or above it must be fully struck. (Unless the coin is usually softly struck such as the Mercury Dime or Standing Liberty Quarter.) Most coins should be graded down to an MS-63 if they are poorly struck and have mushy definition, even if they are mark-free with nice mint luster.

Invest in the best strike available for the specific coin you are purchasing. Although they cost a bit more, you are purchasing higher on the supply pyramid and will have a coin with greater appreciation potential.

Coloring Coloring, or toning, is one of the most beautiful aspects of rare coins as well as being an important factor to grading—particularly so with copper coins. Toning is the natural aging process a coin undergoes. It results from a combination of the coin's metallic content, the storage facilities, and the atmospheric content. A brilliant uncirculated silver coin can tone to a beautiful golden hue and bring a premium price. However, it can just as easily turn coal black, obscuring the coin's luster and decreasing its value. Toning must be understood by the rare coin investor so as to properly grade copper coins and to appreciate price differences of similar coins with dissimilar toning.

The following discussion is based on *Color and Toning on Uncirculated and Proof U.S. Coins*, by J.D. Parsons—the best work available on toning.

Copper coins From the time a copper coin is minted, it gradually begins to darken in color. Despite the utmost care in storage, a new cent's red coloring will deepen, the color of which depends upon a wide variety of factors.

Mint red generally deepens into an attractive rose, orange, and gold combination, similar to a sunset. Frequently on Proof Indian Head Cents the rose will continue to darken into violet. Occasionally the coins follow a sequence of turning gold and then light olive, referred to as "sea green." Often on Large Cents the tops of the ridges will turn bluish olive while the protected areas stay mint red, producing a beautiful iridescent piece.

Indian Cents, especially proofs, will tone to a rainbow of colors—violet, rich rose, bluish violet, and greenish gold are some of the more desirable colors. However, the iridescence seen on proofs is different than that seen on coins minted for general circulation.

The toning process and the hues it produces are due to thin films on the surface of the coin, the result of various oxidation processes. The color will deepen in accordance to the composition and thickness of the film. To best examine toning on a copper coin, tilt the piece back and forth under a strong incandescent light (not fluorescent).

Genuine iridescent toning will change color or disappear altogether as the coin rotates. The colors gradually blend into one another and lack any distinct lines of demarcation. The colors on artificially toned coins will not blend gradually into one another.

As the coin's surface continues to oxidize, the light olive toning will slowly deepen into a walnut color and any remaining mint red will turn tan. Both the walnut and tan coloration can continue to darken into a deep chocolate brown. Despite the gradual darkening, on truly uncirculated coins, the mint luster will still be visible beneath the toning.

Copper coinage is usually considered less desirable if the darkening process continues. The chocolate brown coloration can begin as a light chocolate and deepen to a "Baker's" chocolate. Darker colors are accompanied by minor pitting or surface corrosion. Infrequently a virtually Large Cent is seen with hints of underlying bluish toning. This dark color makes it difficult to detect the mint luster beneath the toning, but the luster must be there in order to maintain a strict uncirculated grade.

As the copper pieces turn darker, and duller, often a color of charcoal, they become less desirable to the collector and thus should be avoided by the investor. Under magnification the coin's surface will be rough with little or no mint luster visible.

There is a great deal of controversy regarding whether these dark coins lacking mint luster can legitimately be considered uncirculated. My advice is to avoid such specimens when purchasing for an investment portfolio.

Another group of less desirable coins are those that have toned unevenly. This encompasses coins that appear blotchy or streaked, evidence that the coin was improperly cleaned decades ago. This uneven, blotchy appearance also occurs when someone attempts to tone a copper coin artificially.

Artificially toned coins are often weirdly iridescent—a patch of blue here, a ring of green there. These colors look as though they were splashed on with watercolors. Additionally, these artificial colors will not blend together when rotated under light. The surfaces under the artificial toning will appear flat and lifeless. Reject these pieces.

46

Nickel coinage Contrary to popular belief, nickels are not pure nickel, but rather an alloy of 75 percent copper and 25 percent nickel. Due to this copper content, some of the toning characteristics appearing in copper coinage also appear in nickel coinage, although to a much more subtle degree.

The original color of a newly minted nickel is similar to stainless steel. As the coin ages, a variety of gentle shades will develop. The most common are a rich, lustrous gold, often seen on gem Buffalo Nickels, and a less desirable dull gray (steel color) with a hint of blue. The latter appears most often on Liberty Head Nickels.

Occasionally, nickels will develop iridescent toning, but it is much more subtle than on copper pieces. The nickel coinage will generally be gold or gray with faint iridescent overtones. The most common colors are pink, green, blue, and occasionally violet. Bizarre or brightly iridescent nickels should be rejected as artificial.

Shield nickels and three cent nickel pieces usually have dull, streaky surfaces, even on proof specimens. This is because they were made at a time when the mint had not yet mastered the polishing and striking of planchets with this alloy. Such streaked pieces are not impaired but simply less desirable than brilliant specimens. The most desirable proof nickels should posses brilliant, mirror-like surfaces, often overlaid with light bluish gray or gold coloring.

Silver coins The variety of colors that will appear on silver coinage spans the entire rainbow. Toning results from a chemical process spread out over a long period of time. There is no consistent way to speed up this process without getting an artificial looking coin.

When a coin is kept in an album for many years, the coin's edges darken from being in contact with the sulphur in the paper. This sulphur spreads a ring of blue or green around the rims of the coin—creating a "halo" effect. As time passes, the halo will converge concentrically in toward the center of the coin. The darkest colors will be at the rims with lighter colors inside. The change of color should be gradual with no distinct lines of demarcation. Often the coin will be a rich gold at the center, deepening to a blue, green, or violet toward the rim.

This toning process happens most rapidly on smaller coins. Many gem half dimes and silver three cent pieces are beautifully toned in concentric rings of rainbow colors all the way to the center of the coin. On half dollars and silver dollars, the concentric rings rarely reach the center. This process takes many decades to occur.

The most desirable coins can appear gray at certain angles with brilliant bluish and greenish colors at other angles. Sometimes the gold color will further deepen into a beautiful blend of a half dozen shades of rose and orange. These are the true gems in numismatics because the colors and toning are viewed as a natural aging phenomenon. Most advanced collectors consider original toning as an asset to a coin's value and will pay accordingly.

Less desirable toning on silver coinage includes two main areas: coins with irregular toning (often very distinct lines of demarcation) and coins that have tarnished in areas to a dull black, seen in streaks running across the coin. As an investor, select coins with the greatest aesthetic appeal because you will most likely be reselling years later to a collector, not an investor.

Gold coins   Since gold is virtually impervious to tarnish and corrosion, little discussion of toning is necessary. Gold coins are 90 percent gold and 10 percent copper, and any toning that does occur is a result of the copper.

The majority of uncirculated or proof gold coins are as brilliant as the day they were minted. Changes in color are rare and tend to take longer than a century to develop. Additionally, such color changes are extremely subtle. On 18th century coins, the color often deepens to a light rose coloring, while on early 19th century coinage, a light olive overtone develops.

A final note on toning   Artificial toning is used to hide a wide variety of defects. Carefully examine any unusual looking piece. Look for nicks, scratches, hairlines, minor repairs, soldered on mint mark, altered dates, even filled in holes, and particularly check for wear. Be wary of a vividly toned coin lacking underlying mint luster. Such coloring is almost always artificial, and the piece is not uncirculated.

DEMAND

No matter how scarce a coin is, no matter how flawless its grade, breathtaking its toning, or razor sharp its strike, if there is no demand for the coin, it has no value. Demand is the last factor in determining an investment quality coin. It is the most important, for without it, all other factors previously discussed would become meaningless.

The breadth of the rare coin market in the United States was discussed earlier, with estimates of between five to twelve million coin collectors. Yet within that large and active marketplace, not all coins are met with enthusiastic demand.

Scarcity doesn't automatically merit collector demand, for demand is based on a variety of other, often intangible, factors. An example of demand and scarcity is illustrated in the price comparison of a famed 1804 Silver Dollar and the 1742 "Lima-Style" Brasher Doubloon, both major numismatic rarities. Recently, the 1804 sold at auction for $400,000 and the Lima-Style Doubloon sold for $80,000. However, there are fifteen known specimens of the 1804 dollar and only two known specimens of the Doubloon.

The apparent price imbalance occurs because the 1804 is in greater demand. It is more famous, more romanticized, and more talked about than the lessor known yet technically scarcer Lima-Style Doubloon. If there was no collector demand for rare coins they would quickly return to their intrinsic value. Thus, as evidenced above, demand is the most critical factor in evaluating the investment quality of a numismatic item.

Investment grade coins should possess a long track record of price appreciation. This indicates stable and consistent collector/investor demand. Such coins are "mainstream" or "middle of the road" numismatic items. A few of my clients have lost money by purchasing oddball, lesser known coins that were heavily promoted by over-supplied dealers. These offbeat items not only appreciate at a snail's pace, but investors are faced with other problems such as poor liquidity, difficulty in obtaining accurate price levels, and extremely high dealer markups. The markets are so thin for these items that competition among dealers is all but eliminated.

1742 "Lima Style" Brasher Doubloon. Courtesy Bowers and Ruddy Galleries.

Some of the specific coin groups which should be avoided by the rare coin investor include the following four: coins that lack legal tender status, foreign coins, ancient coins, and colonial coins.

Coins Lacking Legal Tender Status

Historically, collectors have favored coinage that was considered legal tender by the issuing country, or coinage that actually could be used as a medium of exchange. Today many countries issue special coinage commemorating an event or an individual. Such coins are more accurately classified as medals because they are never intended to circulate as money.

Small countries issue such items as a money-making promotional device. Bermuda, the Cayman Islands, Panama, Jamaica, and New Guinea are only a sampling of the countries involved. At the time of this writing, the Peoples Republic of China is marketing a proof edition set of gold coins to be distributed over the next three years by Amwest Financial of Los Angeles. Although promoted as legal tender, they represent a "non-circulating" form of legal tender. Unless China's currency was backed and interchangeable with gold, these items would never circulate as a medium of exchange. China's currency is not backed by gold, and as a result, the pieces are not intended to serve as money.

Non-circulating legal tender coinage appreciates no better than commemorative medals and tokens. In my experiences while working in one of the nation's largest retail bullion brokerage houses, I've seen countless people come in to sell such non-legal tender coins. I've seen those same people discouragingly informed their coins were only worth melt value. Bullion dealers generally melt such coinage into a more marketable form. Refiners charge approximately 5 percent of the bullion value, and dealers add another 5 percent for acting as a middleman. Thus such coinage is actually worth only 90 percent of the metal content if a market never develops for it.

Foreign Coinage

Although many foreign coins have significant potential for price appreciation, they are *not* recommended for the average American investor.

When in Rome, do as the Romans do. A native of Japan would be most prudent to invest in Japanese coins. A native of

England would be well advised to concentrate upon coinage of Great Britain. The largest market for U.S. coins is in the United States. The largest market for Japanese coins is in Japan. The largest market for English coins, of course, is in England.

The huge collector base in each respective country makes national coinage easy to buy and sell. An investor of Japanese coins in the United States would face severe problems in trying to obtain top dollar for his or her coins at the time of liquidation. Additionally, the thin market creates higher markups. Dealers of foreign coinage have little competition and often mark up as high as 50 percent.

At the present time, many of the larger rare coin dealers are promoting foreign coins as the "hot" investment of the 80s. Yet few dealers make any mention of liquidity, of how and where to resell your foreign coinage in order to realize your "profits."

No capital gains will be realized if you can't resell the original investment. Steer clear of foreign coinage.

Ancient Coinage

Greek, Roman, Byzantine, etc., coins present a host of problems to the investor. One major problem is with identification and classification. Additionally, counterfeits of such pieces have been made for centuries and are often nearly impossible to detect.

The problems of a thin market are intensified with ancient coinage because there are even fewer dealers in the United States specializing in ancients than there are dealers specializing in foreign coinage. Dealer markups reflect this.

Recently I was birthday shopping for a friend who was fascinated by ancient coinage. I decided to purchase a Roman coin despite my ignorance in that particular field. I contacted a dealer/acquaintance of mine who had a good selection. I found an appropriate item marked for $40 so I asked how much "my" price would be. He sold it to me for $17. Knowing the dealer, I know that he made money on the transaction. A novice investor might have paid $40 for an item that was probably only worth $15.

In this country the markup on ancient coinage is so high that it is nearly impossible for the average collector/investor to come out ahead of the game.

A recently publicized purchase by Nelson Bunker Hunt of a Greek coin for $1 million briefly captured the imagination of the media, yet collector and investor demand remained stagnant. Ancient coinage is historically fascinating but offers poor liquidity and criminally high retail markups. It is another area to avoid.

51

Colonial Coinage

Collector demand for United States colonials is poor, liquidity is low, and their growth record unimpressive. Interest in colonial coinage peaked in 1976 with the celebration of the Bicentennial and the subsequent interest in our early heritage. However, the same colonial pieces declined as much as 50 percent in value over the course of 1977, 1978, and 1979.

The famous Garrett Collection sale rekindled interest by releasing many colonial rarities that had been held off the market for almost a century. Since that time in early 1980, both prices and collector interest have waned.

Colonials are a speculative area within the numismatic market. An investor can do much better by concentrating upon coins with consistent and widespread collector demand.

Any coin purchased as an investment should be relatively scarce, in high grade, and must be in demand amongst a widespread base of collectors. These factors are the foundation for investment quality coins and it is these coins that have appreciated so substantially in the past and should continue to do so in the future.

QUALITY PAYS

When it comes time to sell your investment, you'll appreciate the factors of scarcity, grade, and demand even more. Quality coins sell themselves. If you sell to a coin dealer, he or she will not have to hold quality coins in inventory for long periods of time prior to reselling them. Due to the quick turnover of high quality coins, dealers will pay closer to the coin's actual retail value than they would pay for coins of lower quality. Coins in poor condition may bring only 50–60 percent of their retail value due to the long time they may sit in the dealer's inventory.

How do quality coins fare at auction? On December 1, 1978, Stacks of New York auctioned the Bareford Collection of U.S. gold coins. Out of 242 lots for sale, 92 percent were graded uncirculated or proof. At this quality sale, the average coin sold at 69 percent *above* its cataloged value. (R.S. Yeoman's 1979 *A Guide Book of United States Coins*.) The Bareford Collection's total catalog value was $627,345, and the final prices realized totaled $1,158,205.

Purchasing quality coins pays in the long run. Paying a high price for that quality is money well invested. Some of the specifics of the Bareford sale are listed below:

BAREFORD AUCTION

Coin Type		Grade	Catalog	Price Realized
1851-C	$1	Gem BU	$ 1,100	$ 4,750
1867	$1	Gem BU	1,200	4,250
1836	$2½	Gem BU	2,000	8,000
1892	$2½	Gem BU	600	4,800
1855-S	$3	BU	4,200	11,000
1869	$3	Gem BU	2,800	9,000
1853-D	$5	Gem BU	1,500	17,000
1933	$10	Choice BU	40,000	92,500
1907 (Hi-Re)	$20	Gem BU	4,500	10,500

1877 FIFTY DOLLAR PATTERN

1877 Fifty Dollar Gold Piece. Courtesy Bowers and Ruddy Galleries.

The Fifty Dollar or "Quintuple Eagle" is a massive coin with legends and devices generally similar to the $20 gold coins of the same era. This tentative issue was inspired by the large $50 slugs that circulated in California several decades earlier as a result of the gold rush. Senator Gwin of California presented a bill to Congress in 1854 to coin $100, $50, and $25 gold pieces, to be called the "union," "half-union," and "quarter union," noting that "the half-union should only be struck for the present."

53

There is a great deal of speculation why it took until 1877 to create experimental pieces for this idea. The most logical explanation is based on the artistic awakening taking place in U.S. coinage during this period, evidenced by the fact that more patterns were made in 1877 than in any other year.

Two specimens were struck in gold and sold at $10,000 each in 1910—the highest price ever paid for a coin up to that time. However, a great controversy followed because many argued these two pieces should never have been released. As a result they were returned to the sellers, and then placed back into the hands of the government.

Woodlin, the purchaser, who later became Secretary of the Treasury under Franklin D. Roosevelt, received as compensation several trunks full of patterns of earlier dates—the origin of most pattern coins now in the hands of collectors.

The $50 half-unions were never struck because it was discovered that their size made alteration much easier than the thinner and smaller pieces presently in circulation.

The only known gold specimens of this pattern are permanently impounded by the Smithsonian Institution and are estimated to be worth over $500,000 apiece.

4

RARE COIN ACQUISITION: FROM AUCTION OR DEALERS?

*I*f the characteristics of rare coins are consistent with your investment goals, you must next decide whether to purchase the coins yourself at public auctions or purchase them from a dealer, relying upon his or her expertise. This chapter will examine the advantages of each method of acquisition—dealers and auctions. On the one hand, although auctions offer excitement, the challenge of competing with other collectors, and the possibility of an exceptional find, they more often lead to poor purchases by the beginning investor. On the other hand, although dealers may be considered a safer source of purchasing rare coins, they too have their problems and, of course, their markups.

ACQUIRING COINS AT AUCTION

Auctions are a place of excitement. For those who have the inclination and time to research and study rare coins, auctions can be informative, challenging, and a wonderful opportunity to experience this other aspect of rare coin collecting/investing. Additionally, the novice can attend strictly as a spectator. Meeting and watching the professionals in action and comparing your estimates and evaluations with theirs can be very valuable as well as enjoyable. And the "novice" may someday be experienced and educated enough to enter the bidding on his own.

The most important reason for the beginner to attend auctions is that the individual has the opportunity to examine a huge assortment of high quality rare coins in an unhurried, low-pressure atmosphere. All auctions have viewing sessions occurring several days before the actual auction occurs. Here the collector/

investor may examine coins similar to his or her own, as well as coins valued at many thousands of dollars—coins the individual might never have the opportunity or money to own. It is only through examining thousands of coins that the "novice" progresses to the "expert"; the auction lot viewing provides perhaps the best atmosphere for this.

Disadvantages

However, it cannot be emphasized too strongly that the pitfalls and dangers for the novices are great and could easily lead to financial setbacks or great disappointments in acquisitions. There are four problems that usually make acquiring coins at auction unsafe and impractical for the novice rare coin investor.

1. *Interest and time availability* Do you have both the time and interest to learn about rare coins and stay abreast of the market? If you're buying your own coins at auction you must comprehensively understand grading and pricing—both of which require time-consuming involvement. Although auction catalogs specify a coin's grade, said grading is often on the "optimistic" side.

   Most investors are not interested in sacrificing the necessary time. This is the same reason you utilize a stockbroker. You don't want to spend hours studying in-depth analyses so you (essentially) hire someone to do it for you. You want that broker's expertise, and you're willing to pay a fee for it.

2. *The size of your investment* If you are only able to invest up to $5,000 in rare coins a year, it isn't economical to travel across the country to auctions in order to make a "relatively" small purchase. If your funds are limited, it makes more sense to let a dealer do the legwork for you.

3. *Investment attitude* Are you comfortable directly investing your own funds? Many people would rather not make their own investment decisions, particularly in a field where they have little experience. If you're going to lie awake at nights worrying if you made the right decision or paid too much for a certain coin, then get into an investment program that will select specific coins and grade them for you.

4. *More than meets the eye* Due to a lack of return privileges and a variety of other factors, it is extremely easy to get burned at auction if you don't know exactly what you're doing. Here are a few of the hazards awaiting the novice investor:

a. *Overgrading* Even at public auctions sponsored by some of the largest coin companies in the country, coins are commonly overgraded. As with a small coin dealer, it is in the auction company's self-interest to grade on the high side when it's a close call. This practice becomes evident when a comparison is made between prices realized for similar coins at two different auctions. Note the price disparity below for coins of similar date, mint, and condition from two auctions held a few days apart in California in early June 1981.

This is a particularly good test because the same dealers and collectors attended both auctions.

AUCTION PRICE DISPARITY

Item and auction catalog grade	Auction-X	Auction-Y	Catalog Value
1899 Indian Cent Proof-65	$ 625	$ 220	$ 600
1909-S VDB Cent MS-63	1200	770	1000
1915 Barber Half Proof-65	3000	1650	3500
1907 $5.00 Gold MS-65*	3100	—	3000
1899 $5.00 Gold MS-65*	—	660	3000

*Similar value and rarity.

An unwary investor might have attended auction "Y" and bid full catalog value for many of the coins without realizing they were overgraded. This often happens at auctions; someone unknowingly overbids on a coin and the dealers in attendance smile to one another, wondering if the bidder even bothered to examine the coin prior to bidding.

b. *Shills* Occasionally dealers consign coins to auction, attend the auction, and take part in the bidding to drive up the prices. If you don't know the appropriate value and whether the coin has been graded properly, this little trap can cost you plenty.

c. *"Crazy" Collectors* Imagine you've examined the lots and found several specimens that would fit nicely into your rare coin portfolio. When the bidding begins, there is a field of bidders, but as the price rises, the field narrows to just you and another person. This other bidder may either be or represent a collector who needs that specific item to complete a set or collection. To the "crazy" collector that coin is worth ten times the average market value, ten times more than you should pay.

If you out bid the crazy collector after a bidding war, and these one-on-one competitions are easy to get trapped in, you'll be paying far too much, and it will take you several years just to break even on that item.

ACQUIRING COINS THROUGH A DEALER

Due to traveling costs, the expertise required to successfully purchase rare coins at auction, and the time and diligence required to attain that expertise, the average investor will do much better in the long run by carefully acquiring his or her coins from a reputable dealer. (One mistake made by the uninformed investor at an auction can neutralize the growth potential of his or her entire numismatic portfolio.)

However, purchasing from a dealer still requires initial involvement on the investor's part because the investor must determine which dealer to buy from, which dealers overgrade, and which dealers overcharge. The subsequent commissions an investor pays are a fair exchange for a dealer's expertise. The 15–20 percent commission is particularly not excessive in view of appreciation potential.

My overriding advice is to spend some time in finding a dealer you can trust and then utilize that dealer in all your rare coin purchases. Once you've developed rapport with one particular dealer, you'll probably get better prices as well.

How to Select a Dealer

To select your rare coin dealer, or advisor, be as critical in your choice as you would be in selecting a stock broker or attorney. The five criteria below should aid in the selection.

59

1. Select a company whose primary business is to provide advisory services in the numismatic field.

2. Choose a company that specializes in the acquisition of high quality coins (not low grade common ones for young hobbyists). A dealer unaccustomed to stocking high grade quality coins may have to pay extra to obtain them.

3. Select a company that will maintain a close rapport with each client, following the client's portfolio so as to give advice on when to liquidate. Additional advice from your dealer should be obtainable in areas relating to coin investments, such as taxes and pension funds.

4. Select a corporation that explains, from the beginning, their interest in aiding you when it comes time to sell your coins. This should illustrate their confidence in the portfolio selections they make for you. A company should provide an offer, in writing, to buy your coins back from you in the same grade as they were purchased for. This reduces the risk of buying a coin graded MS-60, and later finding it was actually AU-55.

5. Does the dealer have counterfeit detection knowledge and equipment apparatus, such as a microscope, gram scale, and specific gravity testing device?

6. Is the dealer a member of one of the national teletype systems, which have financial requirements for membership and make an effort to police member practices?

How to Purchase Coins

Coins can be purchased from a dealer in two different ways:

- Walk into a coin shop and buy something.
- Enroll in an investment program set up by the dealer, catered to your individual needs.

This second procedure is preferable to the first. Rare coin investment programs operate differently than a stock subscription plan; they're probably most similar to a book club.

1. An investor determines what type of coins he or she wishes to invest in. The available variety of types increases with the dealership's size and prestige. A good program might offer the following coin types:

60

Commemoratives

Copper Coins

Nickel Coins

Silver Coins

Gold Coins

Type Sets

Silver Dollars

U.S. Currency

2. The investor then determines how much he or she wishes to contribute each month, or every other month, to the investment plan. Depending upon the coin types selected, most programs range from $100 to $5,000 per month.

3. Upon sending the agreed upon funds to the coin company, they will send you several coins, which total that value. You then have between ten and thirty days to approve the items you have received. This is to insure there is agreement between buyer and seller upon the coin's grade.

There are several pros and cons to these dealer sponsored investment programs of which the investor should be aware.

DISADVANTAGES

- Coin dealers are performing a service for you. Their fee is collected in the standard dealer markup, which will be between 15–25 percent.

- Frequently, investment "advice" hinges upon what that particular coin company has in stock at the present time, not what they feel is the best possible investment.

ADVANTAGES

- Little of your time is spent in purchasing or background research.

- Investment programs established by reputable companies will send coins that are of high quality, accurately graded, and guaranteed not to be counterfeit.

- Because you invest each month in an established investment program, an individual is more disciplined to invest regularly, which develops good financial habits in younger investors.

61

- From a cash flow standpoint, most investors have funds available a little bit at a time, rather than huge lump sums.

RARE COIN PURCHASING CHECKLIST

The following three items are essential in purchasing rare coins, regardless of the method by which you purchase:

○ *An up-to-date price list*   This is essential so as to know if you're being overcharged, or paying a reasonable amount. At present the best price guide on the market is *The Coin Dealer Newsletter*, which is published weekly with monthly summaries. The Monthly Summaries include prices for each date and mint of late 19th and most 20th century coinage.

Subscriptions are costly but well worth the price.

The Coin Dealer Newsletter
P.O. Box 2308
Hollywood, CA 90028
3 months for ....$ 18
1 year for 60
2 years for 110

○ *A grading manual*   Current prices are meaningless if you can't determine whether the coins you're buying are accurately graded. Purchase the American Numismatic Association's grading manual, as discussed in the Caveat Emptor section of this book.

○ *A magnifying glass*   Many of a coin's imperfections, such as hairline scratches, tiny nicks, etc., are invisible to the naked eye. An investor should have a 10-power jeweler's loupe to accurately determine the coin's grade. A high quality glass is recommended and will cost approximately thirty dollars.

Recommended Corporations

Listed below are three corporations I would strongly recommend. All combine accurate grading with the integrity to stand behind the items they sell. Each company also offers monthly investment plans, return privileges, grading guarantees, and complimentary newsletters.

1. New England Rare Coin Galleries
   89 Devonshire St.
   Boston, Massachusetts 02109
   National: 1-800-225-6794
   Massachusetts: 1-617-227-2424

2. Bowers & Ruddy Galleries
   (Subsidiary of General Mills)
   5525 Wilshire Blvd.
   Los Angeles, California 90036
   National: 1-800-421-4224
   California: 1-213-857-5700

3. WGY Coin & Stamp Co.
   142 State St.–Box 1012
   Schenectady, New York 12301
   Toll Free 800-833-6606
   New York 518-374-4741

AUGUSTUS SAINT-GAUDENS' 1907 HIGH-RELIEF TWENTY DOLLAR GOLD PIECE
"America's Most Beautiful Coin"

Hi-Relief St. Gaudens. Courtesy Bowers and Ruddy Galleries.

In 1905 Theodore Roosevelt gave Augustus Saint-Gaudens, one of America's most prominent sculptors, the commission for his inaugural medal. The results pleased Roosevelt so much that he initiated a campaign for Saint-Gaudens to improve the designs of the national coinage.

In a letter to Saint-Gaudens, Roosevelt wrote: "I was looking up some gold coins of Alexander the Great today, and I was struck by their high relief. Would it be well to have our coins in high relief, and also to have the rims raised?"

63

Saint-Gaudens replied, "You have hit the nail on the head with regard to the coinage. Of course the great coins (and you might say the only coins) are the Greek ones you speak of, just as the great medals are those of the Fifteenth Century by Pisani and Sperandie. Nothing would please me more than to make the attempt in the direction of the heads of Alexander, but the authorities on modern monetary requirements would I fear 'throw fits' to speak emphatically if the thing were done now."*

The design was finally achieved and made its appearance in 1907. The relief was incredibly high, almost sculptured, and the date appeared in Roman numerals. It was hailed an aesthetic masterpiece.

Although the coin was a tremendous success from the artistic point of view, production problems began to multiply. Several blows of the coining press were required to produce each coin, a situation not conducive to high-speed and low-cost production. Economics won out over artistry, and the design was changed to a low-relief, shallower format. The Roman numerals, understandable as they might be to the better educated, were found confusing by the general public and were subsequently abandoned in favor of the usual Arabic style.

Roosevelt had felt the mentioning of God was inappropriate on our national coinage and thus "IN GOD WE TRUST" was omitted on all 1907 designs. However, in 1908, Congress restored the motto.

Pictured is the finest specimen known to exist. Graded MS-69, it was sold at public auction by Bowers and Ruddy Galleries in March 1980, for $85,000.

---

*Bowers and Ruddy Galleries, *The Great Collection Sales*, Part II, page 69.

5

CAVEAT EMPTOR

As the popularity of rare coin invest-
ment has increased, a great many coin companies and private
mints have sprung up, offering a host of material branded as investments. All too often such items are not. Years ago, abuses in
the securities industry led to the formation of the Securities and
Exchange Commission in 1933 to protect the unwary stock investor. The coin market, however, has no federally or self-regulated
body, and as a result, the coin market's maxim is caveat emptor
to a degree that would make Ralph Nader shudder.

THINGS TO BE WARY OF
WHEN INVESTING IN RARE COINS

Overgrading

The most common problem in the numismatic field occurs when
dealers grade a coin too high and subsequently overprice it. The
most blatant example of overgrading I have ever encountered occurred some time ago. A client entered our offices with a 1910-D
$10 Gold Piece he had purchased from a local coin shop. The
item had been graded MS-63, and the individual had paid $2,000
for it, approximately $1,000 under the fair market value for a coin
in that condition. The client wished to sell the coin, but upon examination it appeared to have a hint of wear upon it (2½, 5, and
10 dollar Indian Gold Pieces are among the most difficult coins to
grade).

Accompanying the coin was a certification of authenticity
from the Professional Numismatist Guild (PNG), but this service
only authenticates, it does not grade. Thus there were no references to grade on the certificate. However, there was also the top

half of an American Numismatic Association Certification Service (ANACS) certificate, which was the photograph of the coin in question. This indicated to me the coin had been graded by the ANA, but the grade had been purposely cut off the certificate. I called ANACS and, with the original owner's name and the certification date, I discovered the coin had been graded AU-55 and was only worth about one-third of what the client had paid for it.

I imagine that even if the client had been able to obtain a refund, the dealer who cut off the bottom of the ANACS certificate simply resold it to another unsuspecting collector or investor.

The situation wherein lies the greatest danger of purchasing an overgraded coin is when an investor thinks he or she has discovered a bargain. It's only natural to try to get more than you pay for, and on rare occasions you may stumble across a bargain, but shopping for them is dangerous at best. In addition, it's unrealistic to assume that a professional numismatist would sell coins below market value.

It's tempting to buy when a coin is marked MS-60 for $200 and your current price guide lists that coin, in that condition, at $400. What a steal! Look again at the coin. If it is actually AU-55 and "mistakenly" graded MS-60, its real value may only be $100. Paying $200 is far from a bargain.

A dealer is a professional numismatist whose livelihood depends upon profit. It's unrealistic to assume that a professional numismatist would sell coins below the market value. An investor purchasing through greed will invariably pay for his or her mistake when he or she attempts to resell the coin.

When investing in rare coins it is essential that the investor have some familiarity with grading. There are several books on the market that explain the basics of grading for each coin type made by the United States. These include: *Official ANA Grading Standards for U.S. Coins,* edited by Ken Bresset and A. Kosoff (it sells for $5.95) and *Photograde* by J. Ruddy, which is softcover and sells for $3.00.

Several major coin companies are now issuing guarantees of grade with every coin they sell. Essentially, this provides the investor/collector with the assurance that the company selling the coin will buy it back or sell it for you in the same grade you bought it. This is a seemingly obvious responsibility but one which small coin shops do not yet adhere to.

The important consideration for the purchaser of investment quality coins is to be as critical and realistic as when purchasing any other financial security, and to get the grade of the coin in writing with at least a thirty-day return privilege.

The certificate of authenticity appearing on the following page is one I developed while working with C. Rhyne & Associates. At the time of this writing it is the most sophisticated in the field, providing the investor with a money back guarantee in regard to the coin's genuineness, a thirty-day return privilege, a veritable fingerprint of the coin, and most importantly, the coin's grade, in writing. Hopefully, more rare coin companies will provide investors with such guarantees so that fewer people will lose their investment capital as did the client with the 1910-D $10 Gold Piece.

The situation where investors lose their investment capital appears frequently because few people, investors or collectors, can accurately and consistently grade coins. In a conversation with a major Southern Californian dealer, I was told it takes twenty years to learn how to consistently grade coins. This particular dealer is well known for his exaggerations. With diligence, one could learn in ten years.

Many dealers purposely overgrade because too many individuals buy out of ignorance. Despite the existence of a standard grading scale and detailed information pertaining to grading being readily available in the marketplace, grading will always be a slightly arbitrary process. One dealer's "Choice Uncirculated" can be another's "Almost Uncirculated." This discussion will give dealers the benefit of the doubt and assume that any overgrading that occurs in the retail level is done so by honest judgmental error. However, the investor must understand grading so as to know the precise condition of the coin he or she is purchasing. A coin that is overgraded is just that, no value judgments should be made against the seller. But an awareness that overgrading exists can save the investor undue heartache years later.

Counterfeiting

Counterfeiting first appeared around 400 B.C. in Asia Minor, only 300 years after the process of minting coins was established in the region. In this case the counterfeiters merely passed coins of debased metal for their daily expenditures. Centuries later, Rome was plagued by counterfeiters and the largest culprit was Emperor Nero. Nero's coinage looked like the coinage of his prede-

C. Rhyne & Associates
Numismatics Department
Transfer of Title, Guarantee of Authenticity,
and Registration

John
C. Rhyne & Associates, the undersigned, (hereafter referred to as seller) does, hereby sell, trade or otherwise transfer to Armstrong
of 4000 Maple Lane, Anytown, NY 10028
(hereinafter referred to as Purchaser) the numismatic item described as follows for the sum or agreed value of $ 1950.00 . C. Rhyne &
Associates does hereby unconditionally guarantee:

a) That the numismatic item described is legally held and owned by C. Rhyne & Associates, or that C. Rhyne & Associates is acting as the bonafide Selling agent of said owner.

b) That the numismatic item is genuine.

c) That a copy of this instrument will be maintained by C. Rhyne & Associates.

Item: Coin (X); Token ( ); Medal ( ); Bank Note ( ).

Country USA Date 1893 Denomination Commemorative Quarter
Mint Philadelphia Type Isabella Metal Silver Diameter (in.) 24.3mm
Edge Reeded Weight (Grams) 6.25
Impression:Proof ( ) Business Strike (X) Other ( )

The above described item can be more specifically identified by the following surface and/or edge characteristics:

EXPLANATION

AM — Adjustment Marks   S — Scratch or Cut
LM — Lint Marks   B — Bruise or Dent
PF — Planchet Flaw   C — Corrosion or Pitting
N — Nicks   P — Hole, Puncture, or Plug
DB — Die Break

Toning, Staining or Coloring Beginning to tone at periphery

Bag Marked (serious)

It is the opinion of C. Rhyne & Associates, in conjunction with grading guidelines established by the AMERICAN NUMISMATIC ASSOCIATION, that the above described coin has a grade of MS-65 . C. Rhyne & Associates will honor said opinion in the event of resale to C. Rhyne & Associates.

Inventory Number 17-42
Invoice Number 97201

The preparation, execution and delivery of this certificate of the Seller constitutes a representation by him that the information contained herein is according to the best of his knowledge, information and belief. The acceptance of this completed form by the Purchaser indicates his agreement with the information contained herein, although, said Purchaser has a 30 day return privilege from the date of invoice, designated below.

Rights of the Purchaser contained in this document may be assigned or transferred from said Purchaser by the sale of the item described.

Dated this 14th day of October , 1982

Numismatics Manager
C. Rhyne & Associates
110 Cherry Street
Seattle, Washington 98104

Certificate of Authenticity and Grade. Courtesy C. Rhyne & Associates.

cessors, and was the same size, but it was lighter, containing less metal. Technically, he was debasing the currency, causing inflation.

Later, in England during the 12th century, the majority of the King's coiners were found guilty of debasing the currency, and as punishment, their right hands were cut off. However, the problem only grew worse. By the late 1700s, it is said that two-thirds of the coins in England were counterfeit.

Counterfeiting today is a serious problem to the investor or collector. Crude counterfeits made centuries ago are easily detected, but with today's technology at the counterfeiters' disposal, their forgeries are getting harder and harder to detect.

Counterfeit gold coins This section will concentrate upon counterfeit gold coins. These are the easiest to make and the most profitable for the counterfeiter.

During the 1960s, counterfeit gold coins were made primarily in Hong Kong, Singapore, Lebanon, Morocco, and Iran. Today counterfeits are made throughout the world, with the exception of a few communist nations.

Although an in-depth discussion of counterfeits and their respective methodology is beyond the scope of this book, I strongly recommend that you _never_ buy U.S. gold pieces, particularly those with high value, without a written money back guarantee that the coin is genuine.

Sadly enough, most counterfeit gold coins are sold out of ignorance, rather than in attempts to defraud. Few collectors or even dealers have taken the time to stay abreast of the technological developments and recent discoveries in this field.

The Three Dollar Gold Piece serves as an excellent example. It is probably the most often counterfeited gold coin. Three Dollar Gold Pieces were minted from 1854 to 1889 with a cumulative mintage of around 500,000. It is estimated that less than half of that number have survived, due to their popularity as a jewelry item and the melt occurring in 1934 upon President Roosevelt's orders. Due to supply and demand, the Three Dollar Gold Piece is highly valued (between $1000–$5000, depending on condition). It has the greatest difference between gold values and rarity value. For $60–$70 in gold, a counterfeiter can produce a product valued at several thousand dollars.

One situation sticks in my mind illustrating the number of

Three Dollar counterfeits and the lack of knowledge about them among dealers. Some time ago a client presented me with a group of coins for sale. One was an 1855 Three Dollar Gold Piece. However, the coin exhibited a characteristic found on counterfeits of that year. I explained that the piece was a forgery and that I would not buy it. However, the client was not concerned. He had already submitted the coin to several other dealers and had been offered $1300–$1500 for the item.

This problem is remarkably widespread. I would estimate that at least 50 percent of the Three Dollar Gold Pieces held in collections in this country are counterfeit. In the February 1975 issue of *The Numismatist*, the ANACS presented the following table of the Three Dollar Gold Pieces submitted for authentication during the preceding year. The results are disturbing.

ANACS INSPECTED THREE DOLLAR GOLD PIECES

Coin's Date	Number Received	Genuine	Counterfeit	Percent Which Were Counterfeit
1854	40	25	15	38%
1855	51	8	43	84%
1857	17	1	16	94%
1867	8	1	7	88%
1874	41	24	17	41%
1877	9	1	8	89%
1878	66	33	33	50%
1882	66	2	64	97%
1885	6	3	3	50%
1888	29	5	24	83%

Reprinted by permission of the American Numismatic Association.

As stated previously, the origins of counterfeit Three Dollar Gold Pieces are widespread. During the late 1970s, you could purchase in Morocco any date desired for $50 each and in Iran, prior to the revolution, for $52 each. The practice was quite widespread in South Vietnam during the Vietnamese War. Great numbers of American servicemen purchased counterfeit Three Dollar Gold Pieces for $100 apiece.

One counterfeiter of Three Dollar Gold Pieces signs his or her work by placing the Greek letter Omega (Ω) in the top loop of the "R" in America on the front of the coin. The omega is less than one-half millimeter high, and as of this writing, it has only appeared on coins dated 1882.

Genuine 1859 Three Dollar Gold Piece. Courtesy Paramount Rare Coin Company.

Counterfeit 1855 $3 Gold Piece. Note the wide spacing of denticles on the reverse and the partially clogged denticle on the obverse near the "R" in America. Courtesy John Devire.

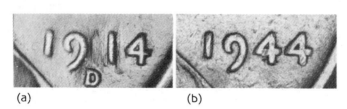

(a)   (b)

(a) Close-up of an altered 1914-D Cent. This is actually a 1944-D Cent with portions of the 4 removed to appear as a 1. Note the tool marks from the removal of portions of the 4, and the uneven spacing of the numerals. (b) An unaltered 1944   Cent.

Close-up of Liberty Seated Dime. (a) A cast counterfeit. Note its crude detail and porous surface. (b) This photo is a genuine. Its details are sharp and clear. Courtesy of John Devire.

A counterfeit $5.00 Liberty Gold Piece. Essentially, a well-made die struck copy. However, on the close-up below, note the raised line of metal above and between the F and the U. This small flaw alone distinguishes this item from an original.

Help for the investor against counterfeits Unfortunately, few collectors and even fewer investors have the time to laboriously study this area. Any gold coin purchased should be certified by the American Numismatic Association. If the coin is found to be counterfeit or altered in some manner, utilize the dealer's money back guarantee *and* make them pay for the certification. I know of no established dealers who would willingly promulgate the distribution of counterfeit coins. Whereas grading is a subjective issue, counterfeiting is a problem that is black and white.

Several excellent books on the subject can help familiarize the investor with some of the more obvious counterfeits. Two of these books are

> *Standard Catalog of United States Altered and Counterfeit Coins* by Virgil Hancock and Larry Spanbauer, published by Sanford J. Durst, 133 East 58th St., New York, NY 10022, $30.00.
>
> *Detecting Counterfeit Gold Coins* by Lonesome John, published by Heigh Ho Printing Co., 3475 Old Conejo Rd, C-6, Newbury Park, CA 91320, $7.98.

The best guarantee one can have to ensure a coin's authenticity is provided by the American Numismatic Association Certification Service. This independent laboratory makes non-destructive tests on coins, paper money, tokens, and medals. ANACS will furnish the individual submitting the item a statement of its opinion in regard to the item's genuineness. The four possible opinions are as follows:

1. *Genuine* A photographic certification will be returned with the item. Fees are outlined in the following pages.
2. *Cannot be certified* This means that the item has been altered, is counterfeit, or is otherwise not genuine. Maximum base fee is $100 plus registered mail fees for return for an item that cannot be certified.
3. *No decision* Occasionally, because of circulation wear, corrosion, damage, or other factors, a definite conclusion cannot be reached. The entire remittance less return postage and registered mail fees will be returned.
4. *Modern replica* ANACS interprets the term "modern replica" to be those items that are made of base metals, sometimes gold or silver plated, and sold as souvenirs or novelties. Only the minimum base fee is charged in this instance.

REQUEST FOR CERTIFICATION · PLEASE USE ONE FORM PER ITEM

R-54321

Name **Armstrong   John**   ANA No. _____
     (Last)   (First)

Address **4000 Maple Lane**   Phone _____

City **Anytown**   State **NY** Zip **10028**

Issue Certificate to: **John A. Armstrong**
(Name or Company)

REQUEST ☑ Authentication Only   ☐ Authentication and Grading
FOR: ☐ Grading Only
     (Original ANACS Certificate **Must** be enclosed)

ITEM DESCRIPTION
Coin ☑ Paper Money ◯ Token ◯ Medal ◯ Other ◯

Issuing Country **USA**

Date of item **1892**   Mint Mark **None** Denom. **50¢**

Owner's value $ **5,000.⁰⁰**   MUST BE ENTERED!!

Other comments _____

From whom acquired **Great Numismatics Ltd.**

I understand and acknowledge that any opinion rendered by the ANA Certification Service on the authenticity or condition of the item submitted herewith represents a considered judgment by the examiners employed by the ANA. Authentication does **not**, however, constitute a guarantee that the item is genuine, and neither authentication nor grading by ANACS guarantees that others will not reach a different conclusion. The item will be examined with nondestructive testing techniques available to the Service and will be judged by examiners based upon information available to them, but no warranties are expressed or implied from any opinion rendered in consequence of this application.

DATE **9-6-80**   SIGNATURE **John Armstrong**

Do not write in this section

Item number _____
Gen. ___ Alt. ____Cft.____ND____
Replica _____ Other _____
Grade-Obv. _____ Rev. _____
Grade _____
Wt. _____ Sp. Gr. _____
_____
_____
_____
_____
_____

RC # _____

FEES PER ITEM

Authentication fee	$ **135.⁰⁰**
Grading fee	**—**
Postage	**2.⁰⁰**
Reg. or Ins. fee	**6.⁵⁰**
Total enclosed	$ **143.⁵⁰**

Make checks payable to ANACS.
Fees are per item—postage may be grouped.

Sample form for the American Numismatic Association Certification Service (ANACS).

USA 1888-S/S Dollar

In our opinion this is a genuine original item as described.
ANACS No. E-4896-G   12-8-80   GRADE: MS-63/63
Registered To: C. Rhyne & Associates, Numismatics

American Numismatic Association Certification of Grade and Authenticity.

All numismatic items received by ANACS are given a thorough testing and evaluation. Each item is given an individual registry number, then weighed and photographed for the ANACS files. The items are then examined with stereo microscopes, and specific gravity tests are performed.

SCHEDULE OF AUTHENTICATION FEES*

Owner's Value	ANA Member Authen.	Grading	Non-Member Authen.	Grading
$ 0–125	$ 5.40	$ 5.00	$ 6.00	$ 6.00
126–250	8.10	5.00	9.00	6.00
251–375	10.80	5.00	12.00	6.00
376–500	13.50	5.00	15.00	6.00
Over 500	2.7% Value	1% Value	3% Value	1.5% Value
Maximum	500.00	20.00	550.00	25.00

*American Numismatic Association Certification Service, 818 North Cascade, Colorado Springs, Colorado 80903

ANACS cannot perform any of the following functions:

1. Estimate value.
2. Describe or attribute any numismatic item.
3. Recommend dealers or other authorities, nor does ANACS buy or sell numismatic items.
4. Authenticate numismatic items on the basis of photographs or rubbings. The item itself must be submitted.
5. Accept responsibility for the return of special or custom made coin holders.

The only drawback to utilizing ANACS is the time involved. Presently it takes anywhere from 10–12 weeks for a coin to be certified and returned to the collector.

One last consideration in regard to counterfeit coins: no coin type or series is immune from the efforts of the counterfeiter, even the lowly penny. A March 11, 1981, edition of "Coin World" described a series of cast counterfeit Indian Head Cents that had been discovered in large numbers on the East Coast.

Altered Coins

Altered coins are genuine coins that have been changed in a manner to resemble another genuine coin of greater value. Two methods commonly used are adhesion, such as soldering on a mint mark, and etching, the removal of a mint mark.

A disqualifying feature might be removed by etching, abrasive reduction, cutting, or grinding. For example, removing the Denver mint mark on a 1922 Lincoln Cent in mint condition would theoretically increase its value by $5,000.

Another, more extreme method, is to join the obverse and reverse of two different but similar coins. This procedure usually leaves a tiny seam around the coin's circumference.

Any genuine coin will stand up to scrutinized examination under a powerful magnifying glass. If the coin in question is highly valued because of a specific mint mark, examine the mint mark under a 10–15X glass. If the mint mark has been artificially applied, it will have dark edges around the configuration of the letter, which may appear ragged and rough when compared to the numbers in the date.

If the outline of the mint mark, or numeral, is not dark and appears to blend with the coin's surface, examine the area one or two millimeters from the edge of the mint mark with lighting from an angle just above the level of the coin. If this surface area appears dished, or concave, the mint mark or numeral is probably the result of pushing the existing metal into the desired shape of the mint mark or numeral. When well done, this can be difficult to detect.

Dates are altered the most frequently. It's a good idea to have an original or similar copy available in order to compare the spacing of the numerals. If the rare coin is a 1914, or any combination of numerals including the number one, check the spacing between the one and the numerals on either side of it. If the coin has been altered, the spacing will be uneven. There will also be minute scratches or "tool marks" where the number four was changed into a one.

Treated Coins

Treated coins are those to which an artificial processing has been applied in an attempt to improve the coin's condition or grade. When purchasing a coin, remember that such a process never improves the fine features of the coin. If it originally exhibited wear, no amount of polishing, shining, dipping, etc., can improve those worn details. The coin will simply be shinier.

Whizzing This refers to roughing the surface of a coin with a small wire brush in a circular motion. The procedure yields minute parallel scratches that appear to the unaided eye as mint luster. A magnifying glass will easily reveal the countless tiny scratches and the artificial luster. On copper coins, whizzing leaves an unnatural orange color.

A coin that is buffed or burnished generally looks "super shiny," but under a glass the fine details are blunted and many hairline scratches are visible.

Dipping   This refers to dipping a badly tarnished coin into a mild acid bath to restore the mint luster. Dipping eats away a thin layer of tarnished metal and, if only done once to a specimen, it is nearly impossible to detect. However, repeated dippings strip away so much of this thin layer that all mint luster is destroyed. The coin appears dull, flat, and lifeless. Under magnification, overdipped coins will appear etched, with ripple surfaces, like beach sand.

Ask yourself if the coin looks right under different lighting conditions and under strong magnification. If you have any doubts but cannot pinpoint the problem, don't buy the item.

Souvenirs

Periodically, coins or sets of coins are advertised in reputable publications such as *The Wall Street Journal* or *Barron's*. The coin items advertised qualify as souvenirs rather than investments. The coins are usually quite common and in average condition.

The Wall Street Journal has a circulation of well over a million persons. Any company running such an advertisement is hoping hundreds of people will respond. If the coins were truly rare, the company could never meet the demand generated from the ad. You are buying very common coins that have lagged far behind investment quality items in respect to price appreciation. The word "investment" is usually not mentioned, and the advertisement stresses everything else. Typical phrases in such ads are, "Encased in a handsomely engraved case worthy of display," or "Something you'll be proud to pass from generation to generation."

If you are serious about rare coin investments, don't buy these items unless you are purchasing them as souvenirs or gifts, but not as an investment.

Private Mints

Avoid new issues of private mints. These have done very poorly in the last 20 years. Although the low mintages of new issues can be alluring, there is very little market for these coins. As was discussed earlier, the thin market and lack of legal tender status make these items a poor place to put your money.

Split Grades

Split grades are usually MS-60 on one side and AU-55 on the other. All too often split grades are sold as uncirculated and can be tough for the beginner to detect.

Coins that possess a split grade will sell at a price in line with the higher grade. However, when you resell it, you will only be offered a price reflecting the lower grade. Always evaluate a rare coin by its weakest link. Split grades have appreciated in accordance to the weak link, not the strong one.

CONCLUSION

Rare coin investments can be extremely profitable, but only if the coins are authentic and are the precise grade you are paying for. Understanding the basics of overgrading, counterfeiting, and altered coins as well as the other considerations discussed may save you a good deal of money years from now.

The following table gives some indication of what the investor is up against.

COMMON ALTERED/COUNTERFEIT COINS

Half Cents:

1793	Cast Copper Counterfeit
1793	Copper Electrotype
1794	Copper Electrotype
1796	Copper Electrotype
1796	Cast Copper
1796	Altered/Pole Removed
1811	Copper Electrotype
1811	Cast Bronze
1831	Copper Electrotype
1836	Copper Electrotype
1840 to 1849	Cast Copper and Copper Electrotypes
1852	Copper Electrotype

Large Cents:

1795	Copper Electrotype
1795	Cast Copper
1799	Cast Base Metal
1799	Altered Date/Last Digit

	1802	Copper Electrotype
	1803	Die Struck (Tool Marks on Throat)
	1803	Copper Electrotype
	1804	Copper Plated
	1815	Plated Cast Base Metal
	1815	Electrotype
	1823	Cast Copper/Buffed
	1851	Cast Copper

Small Cents:

	1856	Altered Date/From 1858
	1856	Cast Base Metal
	1856	Die-Struck Counterfeit
	1856	Altered from 1858/Chased 6
	1858	Fade Proof/Treated and Buffed
	1864	Die Struck 3 Times (Depressions on Beads)
	1867	Die Struck (Common Reverse w/68)
	1868	Die Struck (Common Reverse w/67)
	1877	Re-engraved Last Digit
	1877	Second * Chased to 7 from 1887
	1877	Cast Bronze/Careless Casting
	1878	Die Struck 4 Times (Pimple Left of Shield)
(VDB)	1909-S	Altered 1909/Mint Letter Laid On
(VDB)	1909-S	Altered 1909/Chased Mint Letter
(VDB)	1909-S	Altered 1909/VDB Laid On
(VDB)	1909-S	Altered 1909/S Punched Up and Out from Edge
(VDB)	1909-S	Die Struck (Over 1960 Cent-Traces Visible)
(VDB)	1909-S	Die Struck/Almost Perfect
(Indian)	1909-S	Cast Bronze Counterfeit
(Indian)	1909-S	Letter S Added
	1913-D	Cast Copper/Poor Job
	1914-D	Mint Letter Chased from S
	1914-D	Mint Letter D Laid On
(VDB)	1914-D	Altered Date/From 1944-D

Small Cents:

	1914-D	Altered Date/From 1911-D
	1914-D	Cast Bronze/Rough
	1922	Altered/Mint Letter D Removed
	1922	Altered/Last Digit Chased from 1923
	1922	Cast Copper/Sharp
	1922	Last Digit Laid On/From 1920
	1931-S	Altered from 1930-S
	1931-S	Mint Letter S Laid On 1931
	1950	Fake Proof/Highly Polished Regular
(Double Die)	1955	Die-Struck/Almost Perfect/Import
(Small Date)	1960	"960" are Chased/"1" Is Untouched

Two Cent Piece:

	1864	Cast Copper/Highly Buffed
	(Small Motto)	
	1872	Die Struck (Defective 2)

Three Cent Piece:
(Nickel)

	1865	Die-Struck/German Nickel-Silver
	1866	Die-Struck/German Nickel-Silver
(Proof)	1877	Cast/Altered/Plated and Buffed

Three Cent Piece:
(Silver)

	1852	Cast Silver
	1855	Cast Silver
	1855	Cast Silver Plated
	1860	Die-Struck/German Nickel-Silver
	1861	Die-Struck/German Nickel-Silver

Five Cents:

	1870	Die-Struck/German Nickel-Silver
	1871	Die-Struck/German Nickel-Silver
	1875	Die-Struck/German Nickel-Silver
	1878	Cast/German Nickel-Silver
	1885	Cast Base Metal/Plated
	1900-S	S Added
	1912-D	Mint Letter D Laid On
	1912-S	Mint Letter S Laid On
	1913	Altered from 1903/Cast Case Metal
	1913	Altered Coin/Second 1 Laid On
	1914-D	Altered Coin/Mint Letter D Laid On
(Three Legs)	1937-D	Altered/Leg Removed
	1918/17	Altered/Numeral 7 Chased
	1926-S	S Added
	1939-D	Die Struck Counterfeit
	1950-D	Die Struck Counterfeit
	1944	Mint Letter P Removed
	1944	Cast Silver Alloy
	1950-D	D Added

Half Dime:

	1796	Cast Copper Plated
	1796	Copper Electrotype Plated
	1796	Silver Electrotype
	1797	Silver Electrotype
	1800	Cast Silver/Alloy
	1849-O	Mint Letter O Laid On
	1838	Cast Planchet/Hand Engraved

Dimes:

	1797	Silver Electrotype
	1798	Silver Electrotype
	1798	Cast Base Metal/Plated
	1871-CC	Cast Copper/Silver-Plated
	1889-S	Cast Silver Alloy
	1890	Silver Electrotype
	1891	Cast Silver
	1892	Cast Silver
	1892	Cast Copper/Silver-Plated
	1894-S	Cast Silver Alloy
	1907	Cast Silver
	1911	Cast Silver
(Barber)	1913	Altered from 1943
(Mercury)	1921-D	Cast Silver Alloy
	1916-D	Re-engraved Feathers in Helmet
	1916-D	Mint Letter D Laid On
	1916-D	Mint Letter D Chased from S
	1916-D	Altered Coin/Chased 1926-D
	1916-D	A Clad Process with Reeded Edge
	1916-D	Die-Struck/Almost Perfect
	1916-D	1916 Genuine/Electrotype D
	1916-D	Cast Silver Counterfeit
	1921-D	Mint Letter D Laid On
	1921-D	Numeral 4 Chased to a 2
	1923-D	Die-Struck Counterfeit
	1931-D	Mint Letter D Laid On
(Over 1941)	1942-D	Cast Silver Counterfeit

Twenty Cent Piece:

1877	Cast Counterfeit

Quarter Dollar:

1916	Altered from 1946
1932-S	Mint Letter S Laid On
1932-S	Cast Silver/Sand Finish
1932-D	Cast Silver/Sand Finish
1853	Altered from 1858
1853	Silver-Plated Electrotype
1853	Counterfeit Counterstamp (Puerto Rico)
1853	Cast Silver
1854	Counterfeit Counterstamp (Puerto Rico)
1858	Cast Silver
1861-S	Cast Silver
1872-CC	Cast Silver/Dull Finish

Quarter Dollar:

1877-S	Cast Silver
1896-S	Cast Silver
1909-O	Cast Silver
1919-S	Cast Silver/Flat Details

	1932-S	Letters Chased
	1932-D	Letter D Added
	1932-D	Letter D Chased and Plated
	1936-D	Cast Silver/Buffed
	1964-S	Mint Letter S Added
	1964	Cast Silver Alloy
	1964	Plated and Polished
	1965	Silver-Plated
	1967	Cast Silver/Almost Pure
	1967	Copper Plated/Offered as Pattern

Half Dollar:

	1794	Electrotype/Plated
	1794	Silver Electrotype
	1796	Silver Electrotype
	1826	Silver Plated/Copper Planchet
	1830	Die-Struck/German Nickel-Silver
	1832	Die-Struck/German Nickel-Silver
	1833	Die-Struck/German Nickel-Silver
	1835	Die-Struck/German Nickel-Silver
	1836	Die-Struck/Cast Planchet
	1837	Die-Struck/German Nickel-Silver
	1837	Cast Silver Alloy
	1838	Die-Struck/German Nickel-Silver
	1840	Die-Struck/German Nickel-Silver
	1858	Cast Silver
	1861	Cast Silver
	1873	Cast Silver Alloy
	1876	Cast Silver
	1877	Cast Silver
	1878-CC	Cast Silver
	1878-S	Cast Silver
(Columbian)	1892	Proof/Actually High Polish
(Columbian)	1892	Cast Silver Alloy
	1918	Cast Silver
	1921-D	Cast Silver
	1938-D	Mint Letter D Laid On
	1873	Cast Base Metal/Silver Plated
	1964	Cast Silver Alloy
	1965	Silver-Plated
	1967	Copper-Plated/Offered as Pattern

One Dollar:

	1875-CC	Cast-Silver Counterfeit
	1879	Cast Counterfeit/Pure Silver
	1879-CC	Cast Counterfeit/Satin Buff
	1879-CC	Mint Letters Laid On
	1889-CC	Cast Silver Counterfeit
	1889-CC	Mint Letters CC Laid On

	1892-S	Mint Letter S Laid On
	1893-S	Mint Letter S Laid On
	1804	Silver Electrotype
	1804	Copper Electrotype/Silver-Plated
	1804	Cast Silver
	1804	Altered Last Digit
	1804	Electrotype Numeral 4
(Trade)	1874-CC	Cast Silver Alloy
	1885-CC	Cast Silver Alloy
	1893-CC	Altered from 1898-S
	1901	Cast Counterfeit/Prooflike Field
	1928	Mint Letter Removed
	1903-S	Mint Letter S Laid On

GOLD

One Dollar:

(I)	1852	Cast Gold
(I)	1852–54	Cast Gold/High Purity
	1859	Cast Pure Gold
(III)	1868	Cast Gold/High Purity
(III)	1868	Cast Copper Planchet/Gold Plated
(III)	1856	Die Struck (Weak Feathers)
(III)	1862	Squeezed in Hydraulic Press
(III)	1869	Struck on Cast Dies
(III)	1874	Struck (No Liberty)
(III)	1874	Die Struck (2 Digs on "1")
(III)	1887	Die Struck (Too Large)

Quarter Eagle:

	1808	Cast Gold
	1843-C	Cast Gold
	1843-C	Cast Copper Planchet/Gold Plated
	1843	Cast Gold
	1911	Cast Gold Alloy
	1928-D	Cast Gold Alloy
	1929-D	Cast Gold Alloy
	1883	Die Struck (Heavy Die Polishing)
	1884	Die Struck (Heavy Die Polishing)
	1904	Die Struck (No Reeding!)
	1905	Die Struck (Crack near Left Wing)
	1907	Die Struck (Too Large)
(Indian)	1908	Die Struck (Hairline through Zero)
(Indian)	1910	Struck (No Chest Feathers on Eagle)
(Indian)	1913	Die Struck (No Periods in BLP)
(Indian)	1914	Struck (Raised Rim)

Three Dollar:

	1855	Cast Gold Alloy
	1865	Cast Pure Gold
	1878	Cast Gold Alloy
	1866	Cast/Electrotype
	1854	Die Struck (Weak Upper "I")
	1855	Die Struck (Weak "F")
	1855	Die Struck (Reverse 180 Degrees Rotated)
	1857	Die Struck (Incomplete "I"'s)
	1874	Die Struck (Pimple under Bow)

Half Eagle:

	1803	Gold-Plated Brass
	1803	Cast Gold
	1842	Cast Gold
	1844	Cast Gold
	1846	Cast Gold
	1846-D	Altered Date/Last Digit Chased
(Indian)	1908-S	Cast Gold
(Indian)	1908-S	Cast Copper Planchet/Gold Plated
(Indian)	1909-O	Mint Letter O Laid On
(Indian)	1915-D	Cast Gold
	1891-CC	Die Struck (Weak Scroll under "We")
	1907	Die Struck (Rough Field at "Liberty")
	1907-D	Die Struck (Much Too Large in Diameter)
	1908	Die Struck (Pimples on Face)
(Indian)	1909-D	Die Struck (Obverse Crowded)
(Indian)	1912-S	Die Struck (Faint Periods)
(Indian)	1913	Die Struck (Too Small Diameter)

Eagle:

	1889	Cast Gold
	1889	Cast Gold/Low Grade
	1916	Cast Gold
(Indian)	1933	Cast Gold
	1901	Cast Gold (Crude—Too Light)
	1905	Die Struck (Crude Reverse Denticles)
	1906-D	Die Struck (Heavy Reverse Die Scratches)
(Indian)	1915	Die Struck (Doubling in Edge Stars)
(Indian)	1916-S	Die Struck (Doubling in Edge Stars)

Double Eagle:

	1908	Cast Gold Alloy
	1908-S	Mint Letter S Laid On
(Coronet)	1890-CC	Cast Gold Alloy
(Coronet)	1885	Mint Mark Removed
(Coronet)	1900	Struck with Cast Dies (Crude)
	1910-S	Die Struck (Crude Capital)
	1915-S	Die Struck (Arms Weakly Struck)

FOUR DOLLAR GOLD PIECE

1880 Four Dollar Gold Flowing Hair Stella. Courtesy C. Rhyne & Associates.

The Four Dollar Gold Piece was an unsuccessful attempt to create a coin more suited for international trade. It was suggested by John Kasson, the U.S. Minister to Austria and a former chairman of the Committee of Coinage, Weights and Measures. The intention was to mint a coin with a gold content similar to the Austrian 8 Florin Piece and numerous other foreign coins.

Two designs were produced in 1879, one by Charles E. Barber and the other by George T. Morgan. Barber's Flowing Hair design was an exact copy of a pattern five dollar gold piece designed by his father, William Barber, a year earlier. Originally, 15 flowing hair pieces were struck, but the mint restruck 400 more in 1880 and sold them for six and a half dollars each.

The exact mintage of Morgan's coiled hair stella is unknown. However, David Akers, noted numismatic historian, feels that after the initial ten pieces were minted, a small quantity was restruck along with the flowing hair design restrikes. After examining auction catalogs back to 1882, Akers feels there are between thirteen and fifteen of the 1879 coiled hair pieces in existence.

The idea of an international coinage never captured the imagination of Congress. Just as the proposal had been turned down earlier in 1868 and 1874, the proposal was again rejected in 1880 after the minting of numerous presentation pieces in both 1879 and 1880.

Average values for high quality proof examples are as follows:

1879 Flowing Hair	$ 35,000.
1879 Coiled Hair	115,000.
1880 Flowing Hair	60,000.
1880 Coiled Hair	115,000.

6

TAXES AND RARE COINS

*T*here is much truth in Franklin's statement made nearly two hundred years ago. Taxes are here to stay. However, with a basic understanding of a few simple tax regulations, you can substantially reduce taxes paid in relation to rare coin investment.

Capital Gains

The very nature of coin investment, in respect to the holding period for profit maximization, creates a major tax advantage. Any property held longer than twelve months is classified by the Internal Revenue Service as "long term." Any profit received by selling said property after the twelve-month period is referred to as long-term capital gain. Long-term capital gains (LTCG) are only taxed at 40 percent of an individual's income tax rate.

Therefore, because the highest income bracket is 50 percent in this country, the highest tax on capital gains anyone could feasibly pay is 20 percent. The table below analyzes the effect of income tax on investment income. As illustrated, dividend income (short-term) is severely taxed, while long-term income is taxed at 40 percent of the income tax rate.

FOR EACH $100. OF INVESTED INCOME

	(You Will Receive)	
Your Tax Bracket(%)	Dividends	Capital Gains
32	$68.00	$87.20
36	64.00	85.60
39	61.00	84.40
42	58.00	83.20
45	55.00	82.00
50	50.00	80.00

In addition to the above, LTCG are only taxed in excess of any long-term capital losses that one may have incurred. Since the capital gains tax advantage increases as your income does, the higher your tax bracket, the better a long-term investment will be (from a tax standpoint). This is why many professionals have begun to diversify their portfolios utilizing rare coins.

Classification

The Internal Revenue Service has three different tax classifications for an individual in regard to his or her relationship with rare coins. These are "investor," "collector," and "dealer." The table below outlines the tax ramifications of each classification.

TAX EFFECT OF CLASSIFICATION

IRS Classification	Capital Gains Taxed As	Write Off Expenditures	Pays State Sales Tax
Collector	Capital Gains	No	Yes
Investor	Capital Gains	Yes	Yes
Dealer	Income	Yes	No

As an investor you are permitted to write off expenses and utilize the capital gains tax structure. However, the IRS takes a dim view of collectors who attempt to write off expenses from their taxable income and has taken persons to court on the matter. The expenses that an investor may write off are any ordinary "non-business" expenditures paid or incurred during a tax year if they are:

1. For the production of income.
2. For the management or maintenance of property held for the production of income. This would include insurance, safe deposit box fees, and journals or publications in relation to rare coins.

The IRS criterion for the investor classification is whether one has the profit motive or, according to tax courts, "requisite greed." There are certain basic procedures that should be taken so as to maintain your "investor" status. The suggested actions refer directly to the IRS' criteria for classification. The IRS looks at:

1. The manner in which an activity is conducted.

   Suggestion:
   - Keep a separate bank account for coin purchases.
   - Maintain a business attitude in your coin dealings.
   - Maintain detailed records of your coin purchases, present inventory, and sales.
   - Store coins in a safe deposit box or vault.

2. How much expertise does the taxpayer or his advisor have?

   Suggestion:
   - If a coin dealer suggests a coin as being a good investment, make a note of it, date it, and keep it with your other records.

3. The element of personal pleasure or recreation.

   Suggestion:
   - When speaking to other people about coins, speak of "investing," not "collecting."

4. The expectation the taxpayer has that the assets will appreciate in value.

   Suggestion:
   - When you buy a coin, write down why you feel this is a good investment, date it, and enter it into your other records.

5. The amount of time and effort the taxpayer expends.

   Suggestion:
   - Invest regularly in a specific program, either one you've established or one an investment advisor has.

6. History of income and losses in respect to said activity.
   - This relates to the 1969 Tax Reform Act. The Act maintains that an individual can write off various investment expenses from his or her taxable income if the income from such activity exceeds the deductions from the same activity in two out of five consecutive years.

HOW TO USE YOUR TAX ADVANTAGES

Tax Gain/Loss Switching

Unlike stocks, bonds, and other paper securities, rare coins are excluded from the "Wash Sale Rule" of the tax code. This provides several unique opportunities to the rare coin investor. The Wash

Sale Rule stipulates that a loss cannot be recognized, and thereby deducted from one's income taxes, on the sale of securities where similar securities are purchased thirty days before or thirty days after the loss sale date. Again, this provision does not apply to rare coins.

Two distinct actions can be taken, utilizing this exclusion, which can legally reduce your income tax payments.

1. If you purchased rare coins several years back, you have enjoyed excellent long-term capital gains. When you sell these items you will be faced with capital gains tax of as much as 20 percent. However, if you have incurred long-term losses on other investments in your portfolio, you can use this exclusion to your advantage.

Under these circumstances sell the rare coins that have appreciated and declare the long-term capital gains. However, because long-term gains are only taxed in excess of long-term losses, the two would nullify each other, thereby eliminating your capital gains tax. You can then repurchase numismatic items, establishing a new cost base.

Dr. Richards was a prominent physician whose earning power cast him in the 50 percent tax bracket. During mid-1978 he had purchased a numismatic portfolio valued at $5,000 and it had increased to $13,500, representing a long-term capital gain of $8,500. In his present tax bracket and under present tax regulations, if he sells the portfolio today he will owe $1,700 in long-term capital gains tax ($8,500 × 50% × 40%).

Dr. Richards also sold some Arizona acreage he had held for several years. He lost $9,000 on the transaction. By selling his numismatic portfolio, he declared his $8,500 long-term gain, which was offset by the land transaction. His net position was a long-term loss of $500. He is liable for no taxes on his coins.

Richards made an arrangement with a local dealer so he could repurchase similar coins for only a 5 percent commission, or $675. However, it saved him $1,700 in taxes for a net gain of $1,025 that Richards would have otherwise had to pay.

2. If you purchased rare coins in early 1980, the market's peak, your rare coin portfolio has most likely fallen in value by as much as 25 percent. By utilizing the Wash Sale exclusion, you are able to sell your coins, establish a loss, and repurchase similar items in anticipation of future gains. Although this allows the investor to write off losses, it will reestablish your cost base at a much lower point. This procedure allows you to nullify gains made in other assets.

There are several important guidelines to adhere to so as to properly utilize the Wash Sale exclusion.

a. The sale and repurchase should be executed as two independent transactions on different days so that the investor is "at risk" in the marketplace.

b. The tax code and relevant rulings are not definite on whether subsequent repurchases should be of asset types different than those sold. To avoid challenges from the IRS it is recommended that the investor repurchase asset types different than those sold. For example, sell $5.00 gold pieces and repurchase $10.00 pieces.

Sales Tax

A potential drawback to an investment in the rare coin field is the state sales tax that exists in most states. For all practical purposes this simply increases the price of your coins by 5–8 percent, becoming an additional amount to recover before making a profit.

There are some groups lobbying state legislatures in an attempt to end the sales tax on gold and silver bullion, but even if such actions are successful, it is unlikely the effect will filter down to rare coins. The inequity of a sales tax applied to legal tender whereas it is not applied to stocks and bonds is quite apparent. However, there are several procedures that can be taken so as to minimize state sales tax.

1. Purchase rare coins in states that do not have a sales tax. At the time of this writing there are only five: Alaska, Delaware, Montana, Oregon, and New Hampshire. Unfortunately, none of these states is particularly renowned for its coin companies or auction houses.

2. Become classified as a retail coin dealer (vest pocket dealer) and obtain a retail tax number from your State Board of Equalization. Retail dealers are not required to pay a state sales tax if the items are intended for resale. However, this procedure has several drawbacks:

a. Long-term capital gains are taxed at the full income tax rate.

b. One must make a minimum number of transactions each year to maintain resale status.

c. Many cities require a licensing fee for operating as a dealer within city limits.

For the average investor interested in long-term capital appreciation, this is not the best way to avoid state sales tax.

3. Purchase your coins out of state through the mail. Since the coin company will be sending coins to you out of their respective state, there is no sales tax on the transaction. However, the action of buying through the mail is not recommended unless you are very familiar with the company you're dealing with and you're sure of its integrity and grading standards.

Bear in mind the possibility discussed earlier of overgrading. If you're going to purchase through the mail, make sure the company selling has a thirty-day return policy—don't settle for ten days or fourteen days. It may take you that long just to receive the coins.

If your purchase is large enough, $10,000 and up, and you are well versed in numismatics, the best procedure is to attend an out-of-state auction. Purchase the coins you want and have them mailed (insured) back to your home state. This eliminates the sales tax, allows you to examine the coins in person prior to purchase, and provides you with a tax deductible trip.

If your coin purchases are relatively small, the trip to an auction probably will cost more than the taxes saved. In this case the fourth alternative is the most realistic.

4. Upon purchasing the investment coins within your own state, request the dealer or selling agent to send the items by registered mail to a close friend or relative living out of state. Some dealers will provide this as a complimentary service. Because the coins are being sent out of state, they are not subject to the sales tax.

If your rare coin portfolio is purchased for a corporate retirement fund that is being stored out of state, it also is not subject to state sales tax.

Trading

Real estate agents often advise their clients to trade their present property for the newer property that interests them, plus or minus any cash difference. This is referred to as "trading-up," and it carries with it a major tax advantage. Trading one investment property for another of similar kind eliminates the payment of capital gains tax on the original item.

This applies to rare coins as well as to real estate. Conceivably one can continue trading and continue deferring capital gains tax for an entire lifetime. When the coins are eventually sold, they are taxed on the basis of the original cost of the investment. However, if you wait until you retire, you will be in a much lower tax bracket and your LTCG taxes will be significantly lower.

The Internal Revenue Service is extremely strict in its criteria for "like-kind" property. If you are trading Krugerrands for U.S. Double Eagles, you are required to pay capital gains on the Krugerrands. Since bullion-type coins, unlike numismatic-type coins, represent an investment in gold on world markets, a Krugerrand and a $20 gold piece are not considered to be of the same nature or character. They are not like-kind property and therefore cannot be traded on a tax-free basis. (In the IRS Service Ruling 79-143, property that qualifies as "like-kind" is defined as being of the same nature and character.)

1792 SILVER CENTER CENT

Silver Center Cent. Courtesy Bowers and Ruddy Galleries.

This specimen, the finest known, was acquired in 1923 by John Work Garrett from the collection of Col. James W. Ellsworth. In March 1981, it sold at public auction for $95,000.

Historians have determined that the 1792 Silver Center Cents were the first coins struck at the U.S. mint in Philadelphia. Henry Voigt, the first chief coiner, stated in his account book, "Struck off a few pieces of copper coin," entered under the date, December 18, 1792. A letter that Thomas Jefferson wrote to President Washington regarding coinage reads as follows:

> Th. Jefferson has the honor to send the President two cents made on Voigt's plan by putting a silver plug worth three quarters of a cent into a copper worth one quarter of a cent.

Mr. Rittenhouse is about to make a few by mixing the same plug by fusion with the same quantity of copper. He will then make copper alone of the same size & lastly he will make the real cent as ordered by Congress, four times as big. Specimens of these several ways of making the cent may now be delivered to the Committee of Congress now having the subject before them.*

Frank H. Stewart, a Philadelphia electrical contractor who demolished the original mint buildings during the early 1900s, found two planchets used for making 1792 pattern silver center cents, thereby verifying that the pieces were struck on the mint premises.

Pattern coins of 1792 were made in several formats. The silver center cent was an attempt to reduce the size of the denomination by inserting in the center a silver plug, a metal more valuable than the surrounding copper.

Today there are only eleven specimens known to exist.

---

*Bowers & Ruddy Galleries, *The Garrett Collection Sales,* Part IV, p. 172.

7

RARE COINS AND RETIREMENT

> *We should all be concerned about the future because we will have to spend the rest of our lives there.*
>
> Charles F. Kettering
> "Seed for Thought," 1949

*P*eople are living longer. Your parents lived longer than their parents, and excluding serious accidents, you will live longer than yours. Longer life expectancy has been recognized by the government with the raising of the mandatory retirement age from sixty-five to seventy.

WHY PLAN FOR RETIREMENT NOW?

A recent study of mortality, conducted by Buck Consultants Inc., indicates the typical sixty-five-year-old man can now expect to live to age eighty, and the sixty-five-year-old woman to beyond eighty-four. In light of improved health care and ease of travel, people are looking forward to their retirement years more than ever before.

Most Americans retire when they are sixty-two, so the majority of people will be living on pensions and Social Security for well over fifteen years. This makes financial preparation for your retirement one of the most important investment decisions of your life. All too often this subject is either postponed too long, or never given serious consideration.

The result, remarks economist James Schulz of Brandeis University, is that, "In a very short time, people can go from a comfortable life to the ranks of the near poor."*

Dr. Robert N. Butler, Director of the National Institute on Aging and a 1976 Pulitzer Prize winner believes, "The number one cause of distress for most retired Americans is their income." Economist Thomas Borzilleri of the American Association of Re-

---

*U.S. News and World Report, February 26, 1979, p. 56.

tired People estimates, "About 70 percent of the retired population is barely getting by."*

Why is this happening? One reason is that workers, employees, both blue and white collar, even professionals, rely too heavily on Social Security and company or union pensions. The most obvious reason is that it takes more money to live each year after the paycheck stops.

Consider what a constant 9 percent rate of inflation does to $10,000 of capital. In fifteen years it will be worth only $2,745 in today's dollars, and in twenty-five years that amount decreases to $1,100. That's only 11 cents purchasing power for each dollar you used to have. Those on fixed incomes are always the hardest hit by inflation.

Most corporate pension plans do not have a cost-of-living increase built into them. Thus, these company pension plans are even more susceptible to erosion than Social Security.

Too many corporate pension funds rely on investments that have not kept pace with inflation. Peat, Marwick, Mitchell & Co. surveyed 125 equity funds and found that between 1970–1979, these funds increased at an average annual rate of growth of approximately 3.75 percent, while the consumer price index increased an average of 7.40 percent during that same period. What is sadly ironic is that a recent Lou Harris Poll indicated that the majority of workers enrolled in corporate pension plans view their future as secure.

This is the reason unions are bargaining so hard to gain greater control over the retirement funds of their members. Lane Kirkland, President of the AFL-CIO, angrily stated in mid-1981, "Company-controlled fund investments over the past 10 years achieved only a 4.3 percent rate of return, less than the interest in savings accounts during that same period."

Social Security, on the other hand, has become a precarious house-of-cards, whose very long-term existence is threatened. It is estimated that by 1984, benefit payments will reach 203.3 billion dollars while intake will be 6.2 billion short of that. This condition will only worsen, for as post-World War II "Baby Boomers" enter the age of retirement, there will be fewer and fewer working age taxpayers to support them.

According to the Social Security Administration, while there are presently three workers supporting every benefactor, by the year 2020 there will be only two workers for each retiree.

WHAT CAN YOU DO?

You are by no means helpless to avoid many of the problems mentioned—being aware is the first step, others are discussed below.

1. Start thinking of the future today. The time to start planning for retirement is in your thirties and forties. The old axiom, "You can never start planning too early," has a great deal of truth to it.

2. In the past, most retirement counselors contended that a retired person needed only 60 percent of his or her past annual income each year to live comfortably. Experts are discovering that due to inflation one should use 80 percent as a more realistic planning guide.

3. Women, especially, should plan for retirement or old age. On the average, women live longer than men and therefore will need income several years longer.

4. Develop a regular investment program utilizing rare coins either on your own, or with an investment program administered by a rare coin company, whichever is the more practical. The important point here is not so much *how* a retirement portfolio is assembled, but that such a portfolio *is* assembled.

Individuals can protect themselves from the false hopes offered by many pension funds and by Social Security. As an example, imagine you placed your retirement dollars in an investment that outpaced inflation by 8 percent per year. Due to compounding, $1,000 contributed to that fund every year for forty years would not amount to $40,000, but would have grown to $269,290 in today's dollars.

If your pension fund is like those surveyed by Peat, Marwick, Mitchell & Co., you would be better off with your money in a money market fund, and once interest rates ease back down you would again be losing to inflation. (Not to mention profit taxed as income rather than long-term capital gains.) A retirement fund comprised of rare coins offers a viable and profitable alternative.

Investment in Rare Coins for Retirement

Rare coins are not tax-sheltered In the past, individuals were permitted to utilize rare coins in self-directed pension funds: Individual Retirement Accounts for non-covered employees and Keogh funds for the self-employed. Unfortunately this benefit was eliminated with the passage of President Reagan's tax package (H.R. 4242, Economic Recovery Tax Act of 1981), which was signed into law on August 13, 1981, and went into effect on January 1, 1982.

The provision itself (H.R. 4260, Title 3, subtitle B, Section 314, subsection B, subsection 1, paragraph n) effectively eliminated the tax-sheltered considerations of Individual Retirement Accounts, Keogh Accounts, or other individually directed accounts for all collectibles, including any coin or stamp, any work of art, any rug or antique, any metal or gem, any alcoholic beverage, or any other tangible personal property specified by the Secretary of the Treasury.

This subsection was not a result of intense lobbying by the savings and loan industry, but rather was quietly slipped into the final draft of the House version by Representative James Shannon (Democrat-Massachusetts). The overwhelming majority of Congressmen and Senators were unaware that this provision had been added. Even after the bill's passage, most lawmakers were unaware of subsection 314(b)'s very existence.

The response by hard-money advocates was immediate and swift upon discovery of the provision. Senator Jesse Helms (Republican-North Carolina) stated on August 3rd, on the floor of the Senate, "We show arrogance by pretending to have more knowledge than the individuals personally involved in these plans. We lower the ability of people to care for their own retirement, and we do no service to the financial markets that have been hurt by inflation."

As word of section 314(b) spread, a large lobbying effort was launched by bullion and coin dealers in an attempt to repeal the aforementioned provision. Senator Helms planned to offer legislation to amend the bill "as soon as possible." However, success of said lobbying effort was questionable from the outset. Two major obstacles stood between successfully amending Reagan's Tax Package:

1. *Lobbying efforts were woefully unorchestrated* The vast majority of coin, antique, stamp, diamond, and bullion dealers have a tendency toward extreme individualism, akin to farmers. That stubborn individualism, while in some instances commendable, curtailed the development of a unified lobbying effort.

101

2. *Politics* The major benefactor of the 1981 pension fund legislation, excluding the actual individual, was the savings and loan industry. The increase in the maximum amount contributable, $2,000 and $4,000 for IRA and $15,000 for Keogh, combined with the relaxing of requirements to qualify for said plans channeled billions of badly needed dollars into the savings and loan institutions. The savings and loan industry, represented by a powerful and united lobbying group, had no intention of giving up any portion of their funds without a fight.

Additionally, public opinion was on the side supporting 314(b). Two factors contributed to this situation. First, tangible assets had plummeted in 1980 and 1981. Many investors and pensionees had lost a considerable amount of money and truly believed that such items were indeed unsuitable for a secure retirement fund. Second, the money generated by pension funds was seen as a source of capital for new industrial plant and equipment, a necessity in the drive to increase America's productivity. Because hard asset investments (rare coins, gold, diamonds, etc.) are non-productive in this sense, the business community and the majority in both houses of Congress felt the advantages of 314(b) far outweighed the disadvantages.

Unfortunately, the coin and bullion lobbying effort to amend subsection 314(b) was too little, too late. Hard money advocates were caught "asleep at the wheel," and it will be a long time before tangible personal property, including rare coins, will again be qualified for the tax shelter status within the Individual Retirement Account or the Keogh pension plan.

It is sadly ironic that a Congressional session so intent on submitting to the public's mandate was duped by one lone Congressman and eliminated from eligibility the few items that had proven themselves successful as hedges against inflation.

Rare coins recommended for retirement fund Despite the lost tax-exempt status, the establishment of a rare coin retirement fund is highly recommended. However, surmounting the American tendency to live for today is paramount in order to create a secure retirement. One needn't commit grandiose portions of one's income to develop such a retirement fund. Consistency over an extended period of time is more effective than large sporadic deposits.

102

1885 Liberty Head Nickel. Courtesy C. Rhyne & Associates.

In an age of oil-well tax shelters, real estate limited partner-ships, and commodity options trading, small investors have be-come discouraged with the apparent impossibility of locating sound investments for relatively limited funds. Investors feel trap-ped in an area in which only the "rich get richer." Yet today's over emphasis on highly sophisticated investment vehicles has led many people to overlook a basic factor strongly in their favor— the power of compounding.

The power of compounding is a simple investment process whereby relatively modest amounts invested consistently over an extended length of time appreciate significantly. A substantial growth rate combined with the often lacking discipline to invest on a regular basis produces remarkable results.

Assume an individual invested $100 a month, each month for five years, into gem quality rare coins. If the coins are appre-ciating at an annual rate of 20 percent (they've averaged 27 per-cent in the last 10 years), by the end of the five-year period that investment fund would have grown to $10,177.00.

As the number of years increases, the final sum increases geometrically. An investor with the foresight and the discipline to invest $100 each month for fifteen years, with the same growth rate as above, will have amassed an investment portfolio valued at $111,617.00!

Rare coins are virtually maintenance free and are intended as long-term investments, eliminating the constant buy and sell transactions associated with traditional securities. These two fac-tors make rare coins an ideal investment for personal retirement funds.

THE BRASHER DOUBLOON
(Six Known Specimens)

Brasher Doubloon. Courtesy Bowers and Ruddy Galleries.

The most valuable American coin is the famed 1787 gold doubloon issued by Ephram Brasher, New York goldsmith, silversmith, jeweler, and next door neighbor of George Washington. The few times a specimen has been sold at public auction in the past century it has aroused great publicity and attention. Unfortunately, due to a lack of sophisticated historical records, details surrounding the doubloons are still somewhat of a mystery.

In the latter part of the 18th century, many of the gold coins circulating in America were counterfeit. Therefore it was considered unwise to accept a coin until it was pronounced genuine. The wide variety of denominations, designs, and issuing countries aided the counterfeiters even more. In addition, the problem of clipping (removing small amounts of metal from the coin's edge) and sweating gold coins to reduce their content plagued merchants and tradesmen.

It is believed that Ephram Brasher was called upon to assay, test, and evaluate many of these gold coins. Once this was completed, Brasher would counterstamp the coins with the letters "EB" encased in a small oval-shaped circle. Several foreign gold coins are known today with the EB counterstamp: a guinea of George III and a quarter guinea of George I.

The 1787 doubloons, which bear Brasher's surname in full as a signature, BRASHER, bear no mark of value. This was not unusual. Even when the U.S. mint produced gold coins in the following decade, the pieces carried no mark of denomination. (The same characteristic applied to many foreign coins circulating in that era.) The value of gold coins was determined by their weight and fineness. The EB mark was in effect a guarantee of the coin's quality.

Three distinct theories exist to explain the creation of the Brasher Doubloons. The first, presented by Don Taxay in *The Comprehensive Catalogue and Encyclopedia of United States Coins*, asserts that the pieces were patterns presented to the legislature for proposed copper coinage. This theory has credibility because of the similarity in size between the doubloons and early coppers. On April 20, 1787, the New York Legislature passed a bill entitled, "An Act to Regulate the Circulation of Copper Coins in this State."

The second theory is supported by Wayte Raymond in *The Standard Catalogue of United States Coins*. It proposes that gold coinage was necessary for larger transactions and that the doubloons were minted for this purpose. Another theory contends the pieces were simply made as souvenirs.

Whatever the rationale for minting the pieces, Brasher's doubloons are the most highly prized U.S. coins. The auction records below indicate the value of the items as well as the infrequency of their appearance on the market.

BRASHER DOUBLOON AUCTION RECORDS

Year	Value
1882	$ 505.
1922	3,000.
1978	425,000.
1979	725,000.*
1981	625,000.

*Finest specimen known

For quite some time only five Brasher Doubloons were known to exist, but in the late 19th century, a sixth specimen was discovered in a Philadelphia sewer.

8

RARE COIN STORAGE
AND PRESERVATION

Carefully searching for the right coins to invest in and paying a handsome amount for them are wasted if you carelessly handle or store the items. An MS-67 can deteriorate to an MS-63 when improperly handled or stored. Proper care is essential to protect your investment.

TAKING CARE OF RARE COINS

Handling

While you are examining a rare coin, you should hold it with your fingertips touching only the rim of the coin, not touching the surface of either side. No coin, regardless of its condition, should be held in any other way.

Proof coins are especially susceptible to fingerprints due to the mirror-like surface the coins have. Oil, which is invisible to the eye, will stay with a proof coin for years. Trying to wipe it off will only spread the oil around, causing the coin to discolor years later. There are many 100-year-old proof coins with fingerprints permanently on the field because someone, sometime, touched that area.

While a coin is being examined, felt or another soft material should be placed directly beneath it. In this way, if you should accidently drop the coin, it will not be nicked or scratched.

Do not hold a coin near, or directly under, your mouth when speaking. Small drops of moisture may land on the coin, and these can develop tiny pinpoints of oxidation, referred to as "flyspecks."

Storage

In our atmosphere, metals are constantly under attack by oxygen and moisture, in addition to man-made pollutants in the air, such as sulphur and nitrogen. The corrosion resulting from this attack can cause "spotting," "pitting," "streaking," and "tarnish." Any of these symptoms can reduce a coin's value by 50 percent or more. However, proper storage can maintain your coins in their original condition.

1. *Location* Your storage facility should not be excessively damp. The room's humidity level should be no more than 40 percent. To guard against possible damage in humid areas, you can purchase dehumidifying bags, which will absorb dampness. These bags contain potassium dichromate crystals or silica gel. De-humidifying bags can be purchased in photographic supply stores.

   The best location for an investor to store coins is in the safe deposit boxes available at most savings institutions. These are available for minimal fees and sometimes no charge at all as part of promotional campaigns designed to attract new depositors.

2. *Containers* The container that actually holds the coin must be made of a substance that does not chemically react with the coin's surface.

   There are several common holders for young hobbyists that should *not* be used for investment quality coins: 2×2 paper envelopes and cardboard albums in which the coin is forced into a slot. Both of these holders contain sulphur—which will tarnish the coins over an extended period of time. Sometimes this causes beautiful toning, other times it causes dark and spotty discoloration.

   There are, however, plastic holders that are chemically inert—those that will not react with a coin's surface. These are composed either of polyethylene, ethylcellulose or polystyrene. One of the best containers is the non-acidic Plexiglas holder marketed through Capital, a coin supply manufacturer. Although they are the most expensive containers on the market, about $2.00, they are considered the safest and strongest. They can be purchased in any retail coin shop.

With the proper storage, a high grade investment quality coin will remain so, whether held twenty months or twenty years.

Cleaning Coins

Stop. Don't ever polish or clean a coin with polishes, fine wire brushes, or acid baths. Experts can tell, and you'll devaluate your investment as surely as if you'd drilled a hole through it.

The only circumstance where cleaning a coin is permissible is when a mint set or proof set is fresh from the mint. The minting procedure will leave small invisible amounts of dirt and grease on the coin's surface. This originates from the dies, the presses, or the counting and packaging machines.

If you want to clean new proof or mint sets, take the coins from their original containers and gently wipe them with a clean piece of lint-free terry cloth. Once this is done, repackage the coins in their original containers, or holders of your own choosing. Left sealed over a long period of time, coins with said grease might tarnish. However, this procedure only applies to newly minted proofs, which you shouldn't be purchasing as an investment anyway.

Stick with the maxim: Never clean your coins!

INSURANCE

After investing a sizeable amount in coins it is imperative to take every precaution to safeguard them. Even when safely stored at home or in a bank's safe deposit box, coins are vulnerable to theft, fire, floods, and other hazards.

Insuring your investments against possible catastrophies can be a wise decision. Many investors keep their portfolios at home, confident their homeowner's policy covers their rare coins. Unfortunately, most homeowner policies limit coverage on numismatic property to a maximum of $500.

One of the least expensive and most reliable forms of numismatic insurance can be obtained through the American Numismatic Association. Upon joining the ANA, one qualifies for an insurance policy designed specifically for rare coins. The program is administered by:

Albert H. Wohlers & Company
ANA Group Insurance Plans
1500 Higgins Road
Park Ridge, Illinois 60068

The fundamentals of this particular insurance program are described in depth as folllows:

1. *Range of coverage*   In the event of loss or damage, the ANA Collection Insurance Plan will pay:

   - Up to a maximum of $7,500 if your collection is kept at home or in another location but not in a safe or vault.

   - Up to a maximum of $10,000 if your collection is normally kept in a safe or vault at home or elsewhere. The vault or safe must have a combination lock and a one-hour fire resistant rating.

   - Up to full value if you normally keep your collection in a bank vault or safe deposit box.

   - Up to a maximum of $7,500 for a collection being displayed at an exhibition. This includes coverage for fourteen days prior to and after the exhibition date.

2. *Individual items*   If your investment portfolio includes items, pairs, or sets valued at more than $750 for each item, pair, or set, these must be listed separately with a statement of actual value. You will be reimbursed for the full value listed, otherwise the limit of reimbursement will be to a maximum of $250 per item.

3. *New property protection*   New items added to a collection or investment portfolio will automatically be protected without additional premium as long as the added value is not more than 10 percent of the total insurance presently in effect, or $1000, whichever is less. At the renewal date, your total insurance coverage must be reviewed and your policy adjusted for the additional coverage.

4. *Cost*   The cost of insurance varies with the amount your portfolio is worth and where that portfolio is stored.

   - $1.50 per $100 of value for coins not in a vault or safe.

   - $1.25 per $100 of value for coins kept in a vault or safe at home.

   - $1.00 per $100 of value for coins stored in a bank's safe deposit boxes or vault.

   - $0.50 per $100 of value for coins stored in a safe deposit box with a portfolio valued above $10,000.

   - Premiums are paid annually.

   - Premiums are subject to a 3 percent state premium tax, and minors are not eligible to apply.

111

ANA sample insurance form. Courtesy of the ANA.

5. *Limitations and restrictions*   In order to qualify for the ANA insurance plan you must be a member. Information pertaining to membership can be obtained by writing:

American Numismatic Association
P.O. Box 2366
Colorado Springs, Colorado 80901

Other limitations within the insurance coverage described are listed below:

- Articles are not insured against mysterious disappearance.

- In the event of loss of a pair or set, reimbursement will not exceed the market value of the whole set, less the market value of the balance of the set at the time of the loss.

- Property in transit is covered only if shipped by registered mail or insured parcel post. Property left unattended or in an unoccupied automobile is not covered.

- ANA protection covers collections anywhere in the continental United States, Puerto Rico, Hawaii, and Canada.

- The ANA insurance program is not available to dealers; it is only for investors and collectors.

Insurance may not be necessary if your coins are stored in a bank's safe deposit box because safe deposit boxes are rarely burglarized and are immune from most natural disasters. However, if you do wish to insure numismatic items stored in a bank vault, I would recommend "vault-insurance" offered by Aetna Life & Casualty. Annual rates are 50¢ for each $1000 of coverage with a minimum yearly premium of $25.

1792 HALF-DISME

1792 Silver Half-Disme. Courtesy Bowers and Ruddy Galleries.

The coinage of 1792 had its beginnings a decade earlier. In a report to Congress on January 15, 1782, Robert Morris, Superintendent of Finance, proposed a national coinage. On February 21st, 1782, suggestions for a government mint were approved. However, despite Morris' efforts, the mint was never established.

113

In 1785 Congress gave its approval to the dollar as a basic currency unit with decimal subdivisions, yet still no action was taken to create a mint.

Five years later, in 1790, Congress instructed Secretary of the Treasury Alexander Hamilton to prepare a plan for the establishment of a national mint. Finally, on March 3rd, 1790, President George Washington approved a joint resolution of Congress to establish a coining facility. However, it took several years to establish the facility.

In Washington's fourth annual address on November 6, 1792, he mentioned that coinage had begun. "There has been a small beginning in the coinage of half-dismes; the want of small coins in circulation calling the first attention to them." Interestingly enough, the first coinage of 1792 did not take place at the mint.

It is believed by numismatic historians that the initial production of 1792 Half-Dismes took place in John Harper's cellar at Sixth and Cherry Streets or at another coining facility in a coach house on Sixth Street. Harper was a New Jersey sawmaker with premises in Philadelphia. He worked with government officials off and on during 1792.

During this time, Albion Cox, assayer of the mint, and Henry Voigt, chief coiner, had not yet posted the bonds that, in accordance with law, would enable them to make coins in precious metals—gold and silver. The bonding was such a problem that no silver or gold coins were made during that first year.

The outside minting of the Half-Dismes is substantiated by a document located by Walter Breen. Dated April 9, 1844, the statement of J.R. McClintock, a Treasury official, notes:

> In a conversation with Mr. Adam Eckfeldt today at the mint, he informed me that the Half-Dismes . . . were struck at the request of General Washington to the extent of One Hundred Dollars which sum he deposited in Bullion or Specie for the purpose—the Mint was not at that time fully ready for going into operation—the coining machinery was in the cellar of Mr. Harper's, saw maker at the corner of Cherry and 6th streets, at which place these pieces were struck.

All specimens of the 1792 Half-Disme are circulated, ranging in value from $20,000 to $40,000 for AU specimens. With between 1500–2000 specimens minted, it is not a great rarity but it is one of the more historically interesting.

114

9

LIQUIDATING COINS
FOR CASH

*R*are coins enjoy one of the most sophisticated markets that exist for any of the "collectibles." However, despite that sophistication, there is a very significant trade-off between liquidity and the price you receive for your coins. Regardless of the procedure you select to liquidate your portfolio, the general rule is simple: The more money you want for your coins, the longer it will take to sell them.

WHEN TO SELL YOUR COINS

Throughout this book, it has been stressed repeatedly that rare coins are a long-term investment, with a minimum recommended holding period of five years. Most importantly, it has been emphasized that investment funds should be completely unneeded, discretionary dollars, not emergency funds. Forced liquidation means you'll receive as little as one-half the coins' actual value.

The timing of liquidation is also an important consideration. Ideally one would purchase coins during a market slump, or cooling-off period, such as 1981 and early 1982, and sell when the market is climbing to new highs, as it was in 1980. However, to quote an old Wall Street saying, "The only people that buy at the bottom and sell at the top are liars."

Obviously, it is nearly impossible to buy and sell at exactly the right time, but it will be easier to sell your coins, and you'll receive a better price for them, if you sell when there is an increasing rate of inflation and rising gold prices. This is when the interest in rare coins is greatest. But don't get greedy when prices are climbing. To quote another old saying, "Bulls make money and Bears make money, pigs don't."

One minor point about timing: the longer you hold your rare coins the less important the timing of the sale becomes.

116

WAYS TO SELL YOUR COINS

There are essentially four procedures to sell your rare coins. As stated earlier, there is a distinct trade-off between liquidity and the amount you receive. This section will discuss liquidation procedures in detail.

Sell Directly to Coin Dealers

Take your coins to as many coin dealers as possible within your geographic area. Ask the dealers to submit bids for your coins on an individual, coin-by-coin basis. You'll receive more this way than if they bid on the entire lot. After examining the various bids, sell the individual items to the dealers offering the highest bids.

This involves some time and effort upon the investor's part, but it's necessary to receive the best possible prices. Some of your coins may appeal to one dealer, while others will appeal to another dealer.

The advantages of this process are that you have control over the prices realized, you're guaranteed all the coins will sell, and you will receive payment immediately.

However, the main drawback in this selling procedure can be best summed up by a statement a dealer "friend" of mine made, "I'm in this business to make money. I'll sell coins for as high as I can get away with, and buy them for as little as I can get away with." Although you will obtain payment immediately, you will be receiving a severe discount. The dealer has no guarantee the coins he buys from you will sell, so he expects to be well rewarded for taking that risk.

Unless you need cash immediately, this is *not* a recommended procedure.

Dealer Consignment

The second method is to consign your coins to a dealer for him or her to sell, acting as your agent. This approach will net you more money because you retain ownership and the dealer is not "at risk" by owning the coins.

At C. Rhyne & Associates, we have a standard consignment arrangement whereby the seller receives 90 percent of the sales price of the coins consigned. Additionally, the seller can provide price ranges he or she wishes to attain.

117

Such an arrangement is advantageous because an investor will receive 90 percent of retail, rather than a similar percentage of wholesale. However, the drawback to this liquidation method is the time factor involved. There is no guarantee your coins will sell, and it is only human nature for a dealer to try to sell his or her own inventory prior to selling consigned merchandise.

Coin Shows

The third possibility for an investor to sell his or her coins, particularly an investor who has acquired an impressive portfolio, is to purchase table space at a coin show. In effect, you are becoming a dealer for the duration of the exhibition. High prices can be obtained because most of your sales will be to the general public. Additionally, you will receive payment immediately.

The fee for table space depends upon the prestige of the show, but it usually ranges from $100–$300 for an eight-foot table. For the average investor, this is not a suitable method of liquidation.

Auction

The fourth and perhaps most practical procedure is to consign your rare coins to be sold at public auction, through a company specializing in rare coin auctions. Although you pay the auction firm a fee for its services, this method will net a higher price because more people are competing for your coins.

1. *What can be consigned* Some auction companies deal only with the very highest quality items, whereas others specialize in the lowest quality. Make sure the auction company is suitable for your quality of coins. You don't want your coins to be the best at an auction or the worst, but rather on a par with the other material. (All auction companies recommended at the conclusion of this chapter are suitable for the "investment quality" guidelines discussed earlier.)

2. *Liquidity* It can take anywhere from one to six months to receive funds from coins consigned to auction. Coins must be sent well in advance to the auction houses for processing, grading, listing, photographing, publishing, and advertising. The larger the auction, the more time is necessary because the auction house may be processing several thousand lots.

118

Following the auction there is another delay. Most wholesale buyers have thirty-day payment arrangements with the auction companies, and some clients may simply be late in paying. Also, any successful bid made by mail carries with it a return privilege. Therefore a sale made under such circumstances could easily become nullified.

From the time that consignment is made, it can be two to four months until the auction is actually held, and another one to two months until you receive full payment. However, most of the larger auction houses offer a cash advance against the value of the coins submitted. (Rarely does it exceed 50 percent of the coins' market value.) This enables an investor to receive some funds immediately while still selling in an advantageous manner.

3. *Cost* The commissions charged by auction companies are well worth it. They pay for advertising and beautiful catalogs that attempt to bring the optimum buyer for your coins into the bidding process.

Fees are based on a percentage of the prices realized so it is in the auction company's best interest to obtain the highest prices possible. Fees range anywhere from 7.5 percent to 20 percent.

4. *Prices realized* I personally attended the second Garrett Collection Sale in March of 1980. The market was at an all-time high. Nearly 400 bidders overflowed the auction hall and bid aggressively for some of the highest quality coins in existence. All previous auction records were shattered. Greed and hysteria lifted prices above all rational levels. That was a great night if you were selling, and when selling at auction, that's the atmosphere you dream about.

Occasionally however, the opposite occurs. I speak of dealer collusion. At one of the first major auctions I attended I was shocked to hear several major buyers from the *big* coin companies planning to get together the next morning and go over the auction, lot by lot, literally dividing it up, so as not to compete directly with one another.

In any other industry antitrust legislation would put those buyers in prison, but as stated in the caveat emptor chapter, the rare coin business has no such regulations.

In a soft market, this is the danger to the investor selling at public auction. Dealer collusion can, although it doesn't usually work, seriously cripple competition among bidders. Your coin(s) could sell for less than their fair market value, and because the auctions are "unreserved," you cannot set a minimum, or a floor price, for your coins. However this occurence is the exception, not the rule.

CONCLUSION AND RECOMMENDATIONS

Looking back at the four methods of selling, and the pros and cons of each, the most practical method for the average rare coin investor is to consign coin(s) to a major auction company. Not only does the company present coins in a well-designed and illustrated catalog, but it distributes the catalogs to thousands of collectors across the country.

If you have adhered to the investment guidelines recommended, your "connoisseur" coins will inhibit serious dealer collusion. Coins of the utmost quality excite collectors who bid emotionally to obtain the coins they desire.

Following is a list of the auction companies I would personally recommend for liquidating your rare coin portfolio. They are listed in order of my preference.

1879 Pattern Half-Dollar. Some of the most beautifully designed coins never left the trial stage. Courtesy C. Rhyne & Associates.

1915 Buffalo Nickel. This specimen is unusually well preserved and is graded mint state-67. Courtesy C. Rhyne & Associates.

120

Recommended Auction Companies in the United States

1. Steve Ivy Numismatic Auctions, Inc.
   2121 N. Akard
   Dallas, Texas 75201
   National: 1-800-527-9250
   Texas: 214-742-1079

2. Numismatic and Antiquarian Service Corp. of America
   265 Sunrise Highway
   County Federal Building
   Suite 53
   Rockville Centre
   Long Island, New York 11570
   1-516-764-6677

3. Kagin's
   1000 Insurance Exchange Building
   Des Moines, Iowa 50309
   National: 1-800-247-5335
   Iowa: 515-247-0129

4. New England Rare Coin Auctions
   89 Devonshire Street
   Boston, Massachusetts 02109
   National: 1-800-225-6794
   Massachusetts: 617-227-8800

5. Bowers & Ruddy Galleries, Inc.
   5525 Wilshire Blvd.
   Los Angeles, California 90036
   National: 1-800-421-4224
   California: 213-857-5700

6. Rare Coin Company of America
   31 North Clark Street
   Chicago, Illinois 60602
   312-346-3443

7. Superior Stamp & Coin Co., Inc.
   9301 Wilshire Blvd.
   Beverly Hills, California 90210
   National: 1-800-421-0754
   California: 213-272-0851

8. Paramount Rare Coin Corporation
   One Paramount Plaza
   Englewood, Ohio 45322
   National: 1-800-543-2192
   Ohio: 513-836-8641

9. Stack's
   123 West 57th Street
   New York, New York 10019
   212-582-2580

10. Amwest Numismatics
    9696 Wilshire Blvd
    Suite 300
    Beverly Hills, California 90212
    National: 1-800-421-0588
    California: 213-278-1800

Many auction companies develop expertise and a reputation for one particular area of numismatics, such as Kagin's for U.S. paper currency, or Paramount for U.S. gold coins. However, any of the companies listed above are well suited for general material of "investment" quality.

All auction houses will negotiate consignment rates in accordance with the quality of your coins and the portfolio's value. However, the average fee is 10 percent of the prices realized.

A FINAL WORD

One last point should be made in regard to the liquidation of your rare coin portfolio. Far too many investors in rare collectibles pass away and leave no instructions as to how their surviving heirs can best liquidate those valuable items.

A bereaved widow with little or no knowledge about rare coins is an easy mark for an unscrupulous coin dealer. Leave specific instructions (written) in your will, or in the safe deposit box in which your coins are stored, that explains in great detail who to sell them to, how, etc. Otherwise, your heirs will only receive a fraction of your rare coin portfolio's actual market value.

122

1827 GEM PROOF QUARTER
Ten Known Specimens

1827 Quarter. Courtesy Bowers and Ruddy Galleries.

According to mint records, 4,000 quarters were struck in 1827. However, if this was the case, they were undoubtedly struck with dies bearing another date, such as happened with the dollars minted during 1804. No 1827 quarter ever encountered has any trace of mint luster, a telltale sign on a coin struck for general circulation. It is believed that the entire actual mintage of coins bearing the date 1827 were proofs and that only 12 were originally struck.

The ten known specimens are accounted for as follows:

1. Smithsonian Institution; earliest ownership traced to Adam Eckfeldt.

2. James A. Stack Estate; earliest ownership traced to Joseph J. Mickley.

3. Lot number 962 in the 1976 ANA sale.

4. Private New York collection; earliest ownership traced to Joseph J. Mickley.

5. Norweb Collection; earliest ownership traced to Joseph J. Mickley.

6. Yale University; earliest ownership traced to H. O. Granberg.

123

7. 1977 ANA sale specimen; earliest ownership traced to F.C.C. Boyd.

8. Louis Eliasberg Collection; earliest ownership traced to John H. Clapp.

9. Reed Hawn Sale specimen; earliest ownership traced to a Mr. Alvarez.

10. 1980 Garrett Collection Sale specimen; earliest ownership traced to Joseph J. Mickley.

Joseph J. Mickley obtained four of the specimens when he was 28. Upon visiting the mint in 1827 he obtained them for face value—only twenty-five cents apiece! The one pictured above is specimen number ten and in 1980 sold for $190,000.

10

AMERICAN GOLD COINS:
THE SAFEST WAY
TO OWN GOLD

> You shall not press down upon the brow of labour this crown of thorns; you shall not crucify mankind upon a cross of gold.
>
> *William Jennings Bryan, 1896*

*I*n 1961, Robert Triffin had these thoughts about gold: "It would seem paradoxical and ludicrous that the most rational economic system of international settlements conceivable in this second half of the 20th century consists in digging holes, at immense cost, in distant corners of the world for the sole purpose of extracting gold from them, transporting it across oceans and reburying it immediately afterward in other deep holes especially excavated to receive it and heavily guarded to protect it."

WHY GOLD IS IMPORTANT

Despite the dramatic oratory of William Jennings Bryan and Robert Triffin, gold is probably the best long-term store of value in existence. Gold has literally defined value for thousands of years. The Pharaohs of Egypt, the armies of Alexander, the cavalries of Genghis Khan, the armadas of Spain, countless civilizations and empires have flourished and fallen, proving themselves as mortal as the men creating them; yet throughout recorded time, and before, gold has endured. Men still covet it, still travel to the ends of the earth to uncover it, and will still kill or be killed to keep it.

1863 Proof Ten Dollar Gold Piece. Courtesy Bowers and Ruddy Galleries.

126

The stability of any government's currency is measured in relation to gold despite Keynesian economics' deemphasis of gold's role in world economics. Governments discourage their citizens from possessing gold, declaring it a monetary relic of the past, but those same governments desperately cling to their own gold reserves. These countries fully realize that should their own currency fail, gold provides an economic guarantee that vital government operations will continue.

The Soviet Union utilizes gold a great deal to maintain its present trading levels. The ruble is not a free currency and, therefore, Western countries refuse to accept it. Trade deficits must be made up in foreign currencies or in gold. During the Wheat Embargo in 1980 by the Carter Administration, a substantial portion of Canadian and Argentine wheat was paid for by the Soviet Union with gold.

Gold's value was summed up in a statement by Janos Fekete, deputy head of the National Bank of Hungary, made at a conference of monetary experts: "There are about 300 economists who are against gold—and they may be right. Unfortunately, there are 3 billion inhabitants of the world who still believe in it."

Gold's function as a time proven store of wealth makes it a necessity in any well-diversified portfolio. However, investors in the United States who wish to own gold face a unique dilemma. The legal ownership of gold is a relatively new phenomenon: seven years ago the 42-year ban was lifted, permitting Americans to invest in gold. Investing in gold has been practiced in Europe and Asia for generations. (In both areas, turbulent economic and political conditions provide very few "safe" investments.) Some time ago I met a Vietnamese refugee who had paid $10,000 in gold per family member to be smuggled safely out of the country when it fell to the communists.

Gold Confiscation in the United States

It would be relatively easy for the United States government to once again prohibit the ownership of gold. There are a variety of ways the government could claim the right to do so. Many Treasury officials contend that the Secretary of the Treasury still possesses the authority to confiscate gold under the World War I Trading with the Enemy Act, or under the Federal Reserve Act. Congress could enact a new law delegating said power to the President or simply pass new confiscation legislation itself.

Another means of confiscation, less justifiable under the

Constitution, would be for the President to confiscate unilaterally, without consulting Congress, relying for his authority on the Executive's "emergency powers."

Ownership of gold in this country is not viewed by the government as a right, but as a privilege—a privilege it can take away at will.

This overhanging possibility illuminates one of the key advantages of numismatics. If gold were confiscated, numismatic gold would be excluded, providing a means of gold ownership in the face of opposing regulations. In carefully examining the gold confiscation during the Great Depression, it becomes apparent that if a similar event occurred in the future, owners of numismatic gold coins would be insulated from said confiscation.

Gold confiscation of 1933   On April 5, 1933, acting under the authority of the newly created Emergency Banking Act, President Franklin Roosevelt issued Executive Order No. 6102, part of which declared, "All persons ("any individual, partnership, association or corporation") are hereby required to deliver on or before May 1, 1933 . . . all gold coin, gold bullion and gold certificates . . . ." All holders of gold were forced to surrender their holdings to the government, the gold to be replaced with paper currency.

Violation of the order was punishable with stern measures: Up to ten years in prison and/or up to a $10,000 fine, confiscation of one's gold and its forfeiture to the government, the imposition of a "civil" penalty of twice the value of the gold one was caught possessing.

Because the Executive Order specifically stated "all gold coin," it might have been possible to confiscate all numismatic gold, despite its value, if the order had stopped there. However, the order exempted "gold coins having recognized special value to collectors of rare and unusual coins."

Wording in the above statement becomes an important element. Exempted from the surrender requirement were not "owners" of rare gold coins, nor "holders" of them, nor persons who "possessed" such coins, nor even "investors." On the contrary, the order specifically focused on an individual's motives for having rare gold coins, exempting just one classification: "collectors." There is a clear distinction between "collectors" and "investors" in rare coins.

A collector's primary interest is to possess rare coins because he or she enjoys having them for aesthetic, historical, cul-

128

tural, or even sentimental reasons. An investor's interest in rare coins is financial—the investor hopes to make a profit. In Roosevelt's order it was clear the intention was to exclude only the collector.

Subsequent regulations issued by the Treasury Department stated the exemption would be inapplicable if one's purpose was simply to obtain the bullion: "This exception was not intended to permit nor does it permit the acquisition of gold coins for speculative rather than numismatic purposes."

What rare coins were to be excluded? The Treasury subsequently issued additional regulations under the Executive Order that declared that all "gold coin made prior to 1934 is considered to be of recognized special value to collectors of rare and unusual coins."

Rare gold coins cannot be confiscated The motivation behind the initial exclusion and the preceding definition of coins to be excluded is the key to why future possible confiscation would again bypass numismatic gold coins.

It was the Fifth Amendment of the U.S. Constitution, specifically the Eminent Domain clause, which stood between the rare coin collector and the government during the New Deal's confiscation. Although other provisions of the Fifth Amendment are better known—the Double Jeopardy clause and the privilege against self-incrimination clause—it was a mere twelve words at the end of the Amendment that protected the collector. These are, " . . . nor shall private property be taken (by the government) for public use, without just compensation." Because the confiscation of gold was a taking of private property for public use, a just compensation had to be paid.

1901 Twenty-Dollar Liberty Gold Piece in very fine condition. Courtesy C. Rhyne & Associates.

Bullion was easily confiscated at the official world price for gold, payable in inflatable paper currency, but nonetheless a fair compensation at the time. However, the payment of "just compensation" for rare gold coins, which were not part of the monetary system, would have created horrendous difficulties. The government would have had to analyze and determine just compensation on a rare-coin-by-rare-coin basis, at a massive forced sale of unprecedented scale. Roosevelt fully realized the problems involved with such an undertaking and thus purposely excluded these gold coins from his Executive Order.

If a future confiscation occurred, and the government wished to deal with the enforcement problem, there is no reason that Krugerrands, Canadian Maple Leafs, Mexican 50 Pesos, or similar gold coins would be excluded from the ruling because they present no "just compensation" complications. Once again the government could simply use world gold prices at the time the regulation went into effect. Owners of such coins would be hard pressed to successfully prove they are rare because said coins are heavily advertised as the "best way to own bullion" and sell very close to bullion price.

It should be remembered that the government gains in two ways when it can pay market price for bullion coins: (1) by unloading ever depreciating paper currency that is printed at will, and (2) by acquiring in return vast amounts of gold that can then be turned around and revalued to increasing heights.

The lesson in the New Deal's gold confiscation of 1933 is that due to the Eminent Domain clause in the Fifth Amendment of our Constitution, the government would have been faced with an impossible task if it attempted to confiscate numismatic gold coins as well as bullion coins. How likely or unlikely a future confiscation is rides with the economic success or failure of the country. However, if an individual wishes to own gold, for all the reasons initially discussed in the beginning of this section, it would be wise for that person to purchase gold in the form of American gold coins, thereby possessing gold in a form that virtually guarantees exclusion from a possible gold confiscation in the future.

RECOMMENDATIONS FOR GOLD COIN PURCHASES

I would recommend the purchase of U.S. Double Eagles for the individual wishing to own gold, but concerned about the possibility of confiscation; specifically, $20 Gold Pieces minted between 1860–1906 in lower grades: Very Fine-20 to Extra Fine-45. These coins contain .9675 an ounce of gold and have the lowest numismatic premium of any U.S. gold coin. Additionally, they fluctuate entirely in relation to spot markets for bullion gold because of their lack of rarity. The table below illustrates how U.S. Double Eagles move lock step with the bullion market.

Date	Gold Price per Ounce	$20 Liberty (III) "Very Fine"	Premium Above Gold Value*
April 6, 1979	$241.50	$287.00	22.8%
November 16, 1979	389.20	455.00	20.8%
January 11, 1980	598.50	631.00	9.0%
January 18, 1980	708.50	745.00	8.9%
January 25, 1980	820.00	816.00	2.8%
December 25, 1981	401.00	480.00	23.7%

* It should be noted that even Krugerrands carry a 6 percent premium above the price of spot gold.

MCMVII (1907) INDIAN HEAD GOLD DOUBLE EAGLE
Unique . . . One Specimen Known to Exist

Unique 1907 Indian Head Gold Double Eagle Pattern. Courtesy Bowers and Ruddy Galleries.

This is without question the most famous pattern in existence. The front design is similar to that adopted for the $10 Indian, whereas the eagle on the coin's reverse was utilized for the reverse of the $20 "Saint-Gaudens" gold piece.

Don Taxay, in *United States Mint and Coinage*, notes correspondence between President Theordore Roosevelt and sculptor Augustus Saint-Gaudens concerning the coin's potential design. Portions selected by David Akers illustrate the coin's progress:

On March 12, 1907, Saint-Gaudens wrote to the President: "I like so much the head with the headdress (and by the way, I am very glad you suggested doing the head in that manner) that I should very much like to see it tried not only on the one-cent piece but also on the twenty-dollar gold piece, instead of the figure of Liberty. I would like to have the mint make a die of the head for the gold coin also, and then a choice can be made between the two when completed. The only change necessary in the event of this being carried out will be the changing of the date from the Liberty side to the Eagle side of the coin."

On March 14, President Roosevelt informed the sculptor that he directed that the dies "be done at once."

On May 11, 1907, Saint-Gaudens wrote to Roosevelt and reiterated his preference for the Indian style: "Indeed, as far as I am concerned, I should prefer seeing the head of Liberty in place of any figure of Liberty on the Twenty Dollar coin as well as on the one-cent. If the idea appeals to you, I would refine the modeling of the head now that I have seen it struck in the small, so as to bring it in scale with the eagle."

President Roosevelt then replied: "I should be glad, if it is possible for you to do so, if you would 'refine' the head of Liberty for at least one small issue of coins."

However, the public preferred the full figure of Liberty, rather than Saint-Gaudens' preference, so the Indian head design was dropped from the double eagle.

The great significance of this piece lies in the fact that, unlike a few of the other unique patterns, this one is not housed in the Smithsonian Institution or in the Mint's private collection. It is one of the few ultra rarities that can still be owned by a private individual.

On July 31, 1981, this piece was auctioned in conjunction with the Annual American Numismatic Association's Convention. Despite the bear market for rare coins prevailing at that time, the item sold for $475,000.

11

RARE COIN LIMITED
PARTNERSHIPS

*T*he recent surge in rare coin values, and the ensuing coverage in the financial press, has spawned a variety of indirect methods for the average individual to invest in rare coins. One such method is through the utilization of limited partnerships.

A limited partnership is a legal arrangement whereby a group of investors pool their funds to purchase an item(s) that they individually cannot afford, or that they individually lack expertise in. There is usually one general partner who makes all managerial and administrative decisions in regard to the investment. The general partner is paid a percentage for this responsibility and his or her expertise. The investors submitting funds are limited partners, so-called because they lack any voting right, and thus their liability and responsibility are limited.

Limited partnerships are most often used for commercial real estate, railroad rolling stock, off-shore drilling supply ships, exploratory oil wells, and the like. This is because each of the aforementioned items pass significant tax saving benefits to the limited partners/investors.

A CASE HISTORY

Recently, on November 5, 1979, the first major rare coin limited partnership was initiated by New England Rare Coin Galleries, Incorporated (NERCG), headquartered in Boston, Massachusetts. The offering was the first rare coin partnership to be sold on an interstate basis, in accordance with guidelines and regulations of the Securities and Exchange Commission (SEC). Thus the partnership was more comparable to a stock offering.

The concept was heralded as a breakthrough by many financial writers. It received coverage in a variety of publications from

Money Magazine to Venita Van Caspel's *Money Dynamics for the 1980's.*

The partnership itself was a closed-end public offering for 20,000 shares at $500 each, for a total of $10,000,000. (Closed-end means no additional shares will be issued and the fund will generally not be publicly traded.) However, the partnership encountered a great many difficulties, making it both impractical for the investor and, as NERCG discovered by mid-1980, for the issuing company and general partner. As a result, the partnership barely broke escrow, finally raising only $2,000,000, 80 percent short of its goal, despite the fact that NERCG is the largest rare coin company in the United States today.

The agreement itself was quite simple. NERCG acted as general partner, buying and selling the coins, and overseeing all administrative functions. The minimum investment allowed was $2,500 unless for an Individual Retirement Account for which the minimum was reduced to $1,500. The holding period (length of the agreement) was to be between five and seven years, as determined by the general partner.

As stated earlier, the partnership proved to be plagued with problems. Some of these problems would be inherent in any rare coin partnership, others were simply the inevitability of breaking new ground and encountering problems no one had faced previously. The key reasons the full 20,000 shares did not sell were the partnership's lack of availability, and its limited profit potential for the investor. These problems are discussed below.

Problems

Availability   Despite high investor interest at the time of the offering (this was the period in which rare coins were skyrocketing in value), most individuals were not able to buy shares in the partnership even if they wanted to. This was due to two reasons: problems with the sales force and states' refusal to authorize the partnership.

Sales force: Because the partnership was classified as a security and registered with the SEC, a coin dealer could not sell the shares. The shares had to be marketed by a registered broker/dealer, such as Merrill Lynch, or a Dean Witter Reynolds.

This created an internal conflict among brokers. Brokerage houses train their representatives to sell traditional corporate and governmental securities, not limited partnerships. Thus brokers felt uncomfortable selling the document, and due to a lack of knowledge in the area, they were unable to field questions about it from their clientele.

Al Diliberto, President of the Guardian Corporation of Connecticut, which underwrote the issue, explained to me that this was a major problem. "I spent half my time flying around the country trying to educate brokers about rare coins," he said.

The result was that many brokers lacked the motivation to promote the new issue to the public.

Individual states: The greatest availability problem of all, and certainly the most disappointing for NERCG, was that the partnership was only available in twenty of the fifty states. This even excluded California, the largest market for rare coins.

When the SEC approves of a limited partnership public offering, they are not passing judgment on the merits of the investment. They are only concerned with full disclosure—ensuring that the general partner is adequately explaining all the technicalities of the offering, all information about himself, and all the risks of the project. This is considered an objective evaluation.

Once an offering passes the SEC criteria, the offering must then pass individual state regulations in which it is to be sold. These are commonly called "blue-sky laws," written to protect the unwary investor from offerings that promise nothing more than "so much blue-sky."

Although some states' full disclosure requirements are more lenient than the SEC's, twenty-eight states go one step further. Not only do they require full disclosure, but the state actually makes a subjective evaluation on the merits of the offering.

If the state feels the offering is too risky or involves too many conflicts of interest for the general partner, they will not allow that security to sell within their state. (The conflict of interest was the hurdle the NERCG partnership was unable to pass in California.) The conflict essentially arose from the fact NERCG was buying the partnership's rare coin portfolio from their own inventory, and adding a 5.88 percent acquisition fee, as well as selling the coins at the termination of the partnership through their own ·auction company for another fee.

Whether due to conflict of interest or simply the newness of the offering, the NERCG partnership was available in less than half the states of the union.

Limited potential returns Partnerships for real-estate or oil wells are based on favorable tax regulations, either tax shelters or very advantageous depreciation schedules, and are offered to high tax bracket individuals who can benefit the most from them. These tax incentives, coupled with the potential profits, more than offset the front-end administrative fees and sales commissions that usually cost 20 percent of the funds contributed. Thus for each $1.00 a limited partner invests in the fund, only 80 cents is actually invested in the investment vehicle.

However, there are no such tax advantages to rare coins and thus the front-end fees become excessively high. It cost NERCG an estimated $250,000 to put together their limited partnership; $75,000 in SEC fees; $100,000 in legal, accounting, selling, and printing fees; with the balance going to other miscellaneous expenses. (This was much more than NERCG had anticipated or desired to spend.) Such costs, whether in this case or future partnerships, must be recovered by the general partner.

In the case of this specific partnership, only 78 cents of each $1.00 of limited partner invested funds actually went for the purchase of rare coins. The utilization of funds was broken down as follows:

USE OF PROCEEDS

Anticipated Usage	Minimum Proceeds	
	Amount	Percentage
Gross Offering Proceeds	$1,000,000	100%
Offering and Organizing Expenses:		
Underwriting Commission	100,000	10%
Organization and Registration	20,000	2%
Reserves	40,000	4%
Available for Investment	$ 840,000	84%
Acquisition Fees	58,000	5.88%
Actual Portfolio Value	$ 781,200	78.12%

An investor purchasing rare coins through this partnership was paying the equivalent of a 22 percent dealer markup, which translates into a required appreciation of 28 percent just for the limited partner to break even. This all but eliminates any potential advantage available through the pooling of funds. An investor would have been no better off had he or she simply purchased the coins from a retail dealer.

THE FUTURE

Limited partnerships for rare coins are still a viable possibility. (Presently I am involved in developing an offering of $1.0 million, limited to the State of California.) However, for the limited partnership method of investment to be advantageous to the investor, the problems encountered with the NERCG partnership must be avoided.

The pooling of funds and the purchasing of expertise (general partner) is to the investor's benefit *if* the fees for said expertise are not excessive, and *if* there are no apparent conflicts of interest for the general partner.

1933 TEN DOLLAR INDIAN
Mintage: 312,500
30—40 Pieces in Existence

1933 Ten Dollar Indian Gold Piece. Courtesy Paramount Rare Coin Company.

Despite an unusually large mintage for a major rarity, this gold coin is highly valued. The 1933 Eagle was struck early in the year and a few were officially and legally released (in contrast to Double Eagles of that year which were struck later) prior to President Franklin Roosevelt's confiscation of gold, and the subsequent halting of further minting and releasing of gold coins from the mint. The vast majority of the 1933 Eagles were not released and were melted down.

That same year, 455,500 $20 gold pieces were minted, but since they hadn't been released, the government immediately melted them down. One can only speculate if a few were smuggled out by mint employees only to resurface in the decades ahead, just as many of the other major U.S. numismatic rarities have been discovered.

Recent prices for the 1933 Ten Dollar Gold Coin:

1973 Superior Sale	$ 15,000
1978 Stacks Auction	92,500
1980 Boston Private Sale	125,000

12

IN-DEPTH MARKET
ANALYSIS

> *There will never be a better time to buy rare coins.*

Any investment intended to protect an individual's wealth and capital over an extended period of time must be solidly entrenched as an investment, based on the realistic expectation that there will be a future demand equal to or greater than the demand existing at the present time. Increasing demand (or diminishing supply) is the basis of capital appreciation in any investment vehicle.

This book has laboriously discussed an abundance of factors supporting the stability of the rare coin market within the United States: estimates as high as eight million coin collectors and investors, thousands of rare coin dealers, and a long and prestigious history of interest in numismatic items. In addition to these, there are several long-term factors that necessitate close analysis.

The forces of supply and demand that create priceless artifacts from the relatively commonplace objects of yesterday seem a tenuous thread. The increasing appreciation of rare coins, after all, is based on the sole assumption that collectors will continue to pay increasing sums of money for items of limited intrinsic value.

In studying this point, the prudent investor must weigh the past in the appropriate perspective, placing the greatest emphasis on analysis of future trends, rather than yesterday's milestones. Therefore, despite the fact that coin collectors have existed for as long as mankind has utilized coinage as a medium of exchange, an investor determined to maintain rare coins as a long-term store of wealth must examine underlying factors so as to resolve the question, "Will there be a rare coin market, or as great a market, ten, twenty, even thirty years in the future?"

THE LONG-TERM FUTURE OF THE RARE COIN MARKET

Positive Factors for Rare Coin Appreciation

Statistical data, long-term projections, and common sense indicate a resounding, "YES!" There are three key factors that will positively influence rare coins' growth and appreciation well into the next century. These three factors are inflation, shifting median age, and personal income.

Inflation Inflation in its most basic definition is too many dollars chasing too few goods. When the supply of money increases faster than the supply of goods and services, inflation occurs. Inflation was briefly touched upon earlier, and that discussion is sufficient for this book's purposes. It is beyond the scope of this writing to accurately detail the multitude of factors causing inflation.

From a historical standpoint and from a practical viewpoint, as long as money is in the form of paper backed only by the "good faith" of the government, this country, and every other country, will continue to depreciate its currency. Man has never consistently held inflation at bay, and there is no evidence that this long-held tradition will be reversed in the near or distant future.

Due to inflation's continuation, regardless of how slight or grandiose the currency depreciation is, rare coins will continue to appreciate in value. All other things nullified (static coin supply and level collector demand), an increasing supply of money will cause rare coin prices to climb, just as it has in the past, and just as it has with more basic goods and services.

Increasing median age In general theory, as the United States' population increases, so will the number of coin collectors and investors, thereby increasing demand for numismatic items. This concept proved itself true from 1945 to 1980. Today, however, the U.S. population is experiencing a declining growth rate with the birth rate slowly approaching zero growth. Yet even if the future population of the United States were to remain static, the demand for rare coins would continue to increase.

This hypothesis is based on the fact that the population group with the greatest financial interest in investment quality coins is comprised of individuals forty years of age and older. Essentially, younger collectors, although enthusiastic, cannot afford investment grade specimens. Additionally, most parents cannot seriously afford to spend the time or money for coin collecting or investing until their children are in college or self-sufficient. The membership department of the American Numismatic Association states that "Our average member is in his or her early 50's."

As we move closer to the 21st century, and the post-World War II baby boom children mature and medical care continues to improve, the aforementioned age bracket (forty and over) will continue to swell in size well into the year 2020. The following table illustrates population projections made by the Census Bureau of the United States.

POPULATION FORECAST
FOR THE UNITED STATES
(IN MILLIONS)

Age	1980	1990	2000
40–44	11.6	17.3	20.9
45–49	11.0	13.8	18.9
50–54	11.7	11.4	16.8
55–59	11.4	10.4	13.1
60–64	9.8	10.4	10.1
65–69	8.7	10.0	9.2
70–74	6.8	7.8	8.2
75–79	4.3	5.5	6.4

In 1980, the forty to seventy-nine-year-old age group had 75.3 million persons. However, it is projected that by the year 2000, this group will have grown to 103.6 million persons—a 37.6 percent increase in the size of the group that influences coin demand the most.

Of significant importance is the increasing number of individuals living past the age of retirement. During retirement many individuals renew, or initially acquire, an interest in coin collecting thereby stimulating demand for quality coins.

Retired persons, as well as all Americans, are paying more and more attention to leisure time activities as well as hobbies such as coin collecting. The effect of this ever-increasing interest in hobbies is reflected by the continuous growth in membership of the American Numismatic Association, the largest coin association in the country, which is aimed specifically at coin "collectors."

NEW MEMBERS ADMITTED TO THE
AMERICAN NUMISMATIC ASSOCIATION

Year	New Members
1973	3,193
1974	3,695
1975	6,119
1976	4,246
1977	4,026
1978	2,984
1979	4,039
1980	7,071
1981*	9,066

*1-81 to 9-81 membership annualized.

Personal income The positive shift in the median age of persons in the United States would be meaningless if their standard of living and incomes dropped dramatically thereby eliminating available funds for rare coin collecting or investing. India, Latin America, and other less developed geographic areas have high population growth rates, but because per capita income (average income per person) remains stagnant, "collectibles" will never attain the prominence they have consistently maintained in this country.

If the growing number of investor age "baby boomers" are to significantly impact the rare coin market, the per capita income, adjusted for inflation, should increase. Estimates illustrated below, made by the U.S. Department of Commerce, show per capita income increasing by 29 percent between 1980 and 1990, as measured in constant dollars.

U.S. PER CAPITA INCOME
(SHOWN IN 1967 DOLLARS)
SOURCE: U.S. DEPARTMENT OF COMMERCE

Year	Amount
1970	$3,476
1980	4,780
1990	6,166

These three factors, inflation, shifting median age, and increasing per capita income, will exert powerfully positive forces upon the rare coin market within the United States. As discussed at the outset of this book, the supply of coins is fixed, and over the next twenty years there will be more persons, each with more money to spend, bidding upon that static supply of rare coins.

143

These are the forces that will continue to exert upward pressure on the rare coin market and that will make rare coins an outstanding investment in the 1980s and beyond.

SHORT-TERM ANALYSIS—1983 THROUGH 1987

The best way to illustrate the philosophical reasons that make the coming years ideal for rare coin investment is to relay the following fable, understood so well by successful investors.

A fable Once upon a time there lived two brothers, Solomon and Samuel, whose father had prospered greatly and left them substantial wealth. Now, neither brother was foolish or frivolous, and with great expectations they set out to increase their wealth tenfold.

As seasons passed and the brothers had sons, and their sons had sons, Solomon prospered. He had increased his wealth as the fish multiply in the sea, and gave his sons untold wealth, so that they might prosper, and their sons could prosper. All was well in the house of Solomon, and he was praised throughout the land for his wisdom.

Yet as time had lined Samuel's face, his fortune slipped through his grasp as sand upon the shore. The greater Samuel toiled and the more diligently he pursued greater wealth, the more elusive it became. By his sixty-fifth year, there was nothing left of the wealth his father had bestowed upon him so many years ago. Samuel became a broken man, living upon the charity of his children.

Finally, stooped with age and all pride spent, Samuel journeyed to Solomon to seek his brother's wisdom. Solomon, as charitable as he was wise, shared his secret. "The way to wealth takes but one ingredient; yet that ingredient is the rarest of qualities amongst men. It is courage. I have watched you over these long years, Samuel, and you have acted as every other man in search of wealth. Your actions have been guided by fear and greed, rather than courage and vision."

"Courage!" Samuel exclaimed. "I come to you in search of wealth. Courage is but a badge for young men in battle."

Solomon listened and continued, patient as the teacher of small children, "Courage is the badge you have lacked. When your property fell in value and harbingers of doom multiplied, you panicked and sold that property, fearing further losses. Yet

144

the man of courage stood fast and bought, confident the fall was temporary. Where you, brother, saw fear and hopelessness, the courageous man saw only opportunity.

"When a property soared in value, climbing daily to mountainous heights, you rushed to buy that item, as a lemming amongst other lemmings. Yet the man of courage acted thus and sold that property, against the advice of all about him, for his vision was not obscured by greed.

"I have acquired all you see before you by acting with courage, by ignoring both doomsayers and sheeplike crowds of greed-filled men. I have invested with my mind, not my heart. That, my brother, is the only secret to acquiring wealth." For the first time in his life Samuel understood his folly, and his bent shoulders sank deeper.

But Solomon continued, "Despair not. You have squandered all your possessions, yet you have one thing of value to hand down to your sons and that is the words I have passed on to you. Pass these words on to them so they may prosper, and so their sons may prosper. Their wealth will multiply as mine, and your gift will be more precious than all others."

And it came to pass, and Samuel's children multiplied their wealth for generations, and Samuel, like Solomon, was praised for his wisdom throughout the land.

The moral is often easier to comprehend than it is to implement. Buy when others are selling, and sell when others are buying. In regard to rare coins, while rare coins present excellent long-term growth, there are periods in which it is more advantageous to be either a buyer or a seller. The years 1983 through 1985 will present an excellent buying opportunity.

Present situation Between March 1980 and August 1982, the usually stable rare coin market fell between 10–50 percent, depending upon what coin types and conditions were purchased. (The only coin types to increase during this phase of the market cycle were Mercury Dimes and Morgan Dollars.) Admittedly a significant drop, but not disastrous, for prior to that period between January 1979 and March 1980, investment quality rare coins appreciated in value by 400, 500, and some as much as 800 percent! The market had literally exploded and then retreated, correcting itself in line with a more realistic long-term appreciation trend.

Many dealers pointed to this market dip as a freak occurrence, yet closer examination reveals that similar market corrections took place in 1937–8, 1945–6, 1950–1, 1957–8, 1966, and

145

1976 and that this occurrence is a normal part of rare coins' long-term price movement. Historically, the rare coin market moves in cycles, with each cycle lasting anywhere from five to ten years and consisting of three distinct stages.

1. *A period of market inactivity.* Investors are hesitant to enter the market at this time. Prices move sideways, and rare coins can be purchased at bargain levels.

2. *The growth period.* Dealers and collectors accumulate undervalued coins, and prices begin to advance significantly.

3. *Boom/bust stage.* A great rush of investors now enters the market. Prices rise too fast, peak, and then fall, generally 25 percent. The market cools off, and the cycle begins again.

Despite market corrections occurring in the third stage of the cycle, each successive peak has been higher than the preceding peak, and each successive valley has been higher than the preceding valley. Although there is fluctuation between the stages, the long-term trend is distinctly upward.

Specific reasons for the price correction occurring in late 1980 and early 1982 was a combination of three factors: an unusually large number of speculators entering the market, a collapse of the metals market, and historically high interest rates.

1. During the early portion of the boom/bust stage, many speculators (more so than usual) jumped into the rare coin market, driving prices artificially high.

"The money coming into the coin market was, for the most part, new money," says Walter Perschke. Benjamin Stack, a partner in Stack's of New York, adds, "We had people coming in here, pointing to the showcase and saying, 'I'll take this and this' without even asking what they were buying."[*]

The speculative pattern followed previous rare coin cycles and set the stage for a market correction, but two additional factors intensified the correction. As a result the market as a whole fell 35 percent, rather than the historical average of 20 percent.

2. The average rare coin dealer also sells gold bullion coins—South African Krugerrands, Canadian Maple Leafs, etc. As gold climbed in value during late 1979, dealers amassed large, unhedged inventories of the bullion items. However, when gold plummeted from its high of $875 down to $320, dealers were

---

[*]*Speculators Unsettle U.S. Rare-Coin Market,* Wall Street Journal, March 2, 1981.

faced with significant losses. Dealers panicked and, in an effort to cut their losses, began selling off large numbers of rare coins at bargain prices.

3. Additionally, the prime interest rate was near record levels, and the cost of holding large quantities of coins in inventory became prohibitively expensive. This also drew large amounts of investor dollars out of the "tangible" market and into money market funds.

Thus the usually stable and orderly coin market was suddenly engulfed by dealers anxious to cut bullion losses and struggling to reduce inventory so as to reduce their cost of doing business.

The synergistic effect of interest rates and plunging gold and silver prices fueled the normal correction, giving it added momentum. The final result was a market decline more pronounced than those occurring in 1956, 1966, and 1976. Coin prices there-

FORECAST OF THE RARE
COIN MARKET CYCLE

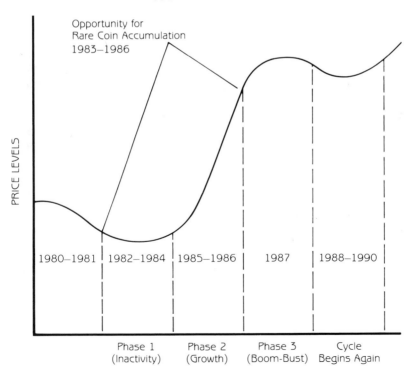

| 1980–1981 | 1982–1984 | 1985–1986 | 1987 | 1988–1990 |

| Phase 1 | Phase 2 | Phase 3 | Cycle |
| (Inactivity) | (Growth) | (Boom-Bust) | Begins Again |

147

The 1877 is one of the rarest Indian Head Cents. Courtesy Bowers and Ruddy Galleries.

upon "dropped back to levels set by long-term collectors," says William Hawfield, President of Bowers and Ruddy Galleries, Inc.*

At present the rare coin market is in a stage varying from inactivity to slow growth. This offers the rare coin investor the best buying opportunity that will exist in the next five to ten years. Looking back, the prices of 1976 were bargains. In 1987, many investors will undoubtedly regret not buying rare coins during the early 1980s, when the prices were so low. In relation to the rare coin cycle, there will *never* be a better time to buy.

CONCLUSION

A lengthy conclusion at this point would be unnecessary. Briefly, however, this book has attempted to explain why rare coins appreciate and how an individual, such as yourself, can invest in coins in such a manner so as to fully maximize your return.

Despite the risks involved, rare coins provide excellent diversification to the average investment portfolio. They offer stability, impressive appreciation, security, and a favorable tax treatment. With the market in its present stage of the cycle, providing unmatched opportunity for the buyer of coins, a cautious investor of rare coins today should do very, very well over the next five years and beyond.

I

UNITED STATES COIN
TYPES AND
DESCRIPTIVE DATA

1. Half Cent (Liberty Cap) 1793

Size: 22 mm
Weight: 6.74 grams
Edge: Lettered
Composition: Copper
Amount Minted: 35,334
Proofs Minted: None Recorded
Mint Marks: None
Designer: Adam Eckfeldt

2. Half Cent (Liberty Cap) 1794–1797

Size: 23.5 mm
Weight: 6.74 grams (1794–5)
         5.44 grams (1796–7)
Edge: Plain—1796
       Lettered—1794, 5, 7
Composition: Copper
Amount Minted: 329,728
Proofs Minted: None Recorded
Mint Marks: None
Designers: 1794 Robert Scot
           1796 John Gardner

3. Half Cent (Draped Bust) 1800–1808

Size: 23.5 mm
Weight: 5.44 grams
Edge: Plain
Composition: Copper
Amount Minted: 3,425,572
Proofs Minted: None Recorded
Mint Marks: None
Designers: Gilbert Stuart
           Robert Scot

4. Half Cent (Classic Head) 1809–1836

Size: 23.5 mm
Weight: 5.44 grams
Edge: Plain
Composition: Copper
Amount Minted: 3,637,912
Proofs Minted: None Recorded
Mint Marks: None
Designer: John Reich

5. Half Cent (Braided Hair) 1840–1857

Size: 23 mm
Weight: 5.44 grams
Edge: Plain
Composition: Copper
Amount Minted: 544,510
Proofs Minted: 1840–9, 1852
Mint Marks: None
Designers: William Kneass
            Christian Gobrecht

6. Large Cent (Flowing Hair-Chain Reverse) 1793

Size: 26.5 mm
Weight: 13.48 grams
Edge: Milled
Composition: Copper
Amount Minted: 36,103
Proofs Minted: None Recorded
Mint Marks: None
Designer: Henry Voight

7. Large Cent (Flowing Hair-Wreath Reverse) 1793

Size: 27 mm
Weight: 13.48 grams
Edge: Vine and Bars; Lettered
Composition: Copper
Amount Minted: 63,353
Proofs Minted: None Recorded
Mint Marks: None
Designer: Adam Eckfeldt

8. Large Cent (Liberty Cap) 1793–1796

Size: 29 mm
Weight: 13.48 grams, 1793–5
        10.89 grams, 1796
Edge: Lettered and Plain
Composition: Copper
Amount Minted: 1,577,902
Proofs Minted: None Recorded
Mint Marks: None
Designer: Joseph Wright

9. Large Cent (Draped Bust) 1796–1807

Size: 29 mm
Weight: 10.89 grams
Edge: Plain
Composition: Copper
Amount Minted: 16,009,810
Proofs Minted: None Recorded
Mint Marks: None
Designers: Robert Scot
           Gilbert Stuart

10. Large Cent (Classic Head) 1808–1814

Size: 29 mm
Weight: 10.89 grams
Edge: Plain
Composition: Copper
Amount Minted: 4,850,722
Proofs Minted: None Recorded
Mint Marks: None
Designer: John Reich

11. Large Cent (Coronet) 1816–1839

Size: 28.5 mm
Weight: 10.89 grams
Edge: Plain
Composition: Copper
Amount Minted: 56,384,561
Proofs Minted: None Recorded
Mint Marks: None
Designers: Robert Scot
           William Kneass

12. Large Cent (Braided Hair) 1839–1857

Size: 27.5 mm
Weight: 10.89 grams
Edge: Plain
Composition: Copper
Amount Minted: 70,918,871
Proofs Minted: None Recorded
Mint Marks: None
Designer: William Kneass

152

13. Small Cent (Flying Eagle) (1856) 1857–1858

Size: 19 mm
Weight: 4.67 grams
Edge: Plain
Composition: 88% Copper
                     12% Nickel
Amount Minted: 42,050,000
Proofs Minted: 280 (1857–1858)
                    1000 in 1856
Mint Marks: None
Designer: James Longacre

14. Small Cent (Indian Head-No Shield) 1859

Size: 19 mm
Weight: 4.67 grams
Edge: Plain
Composition: 88% Copper
                     12% Nickel
Amount Minted: 36,400,000
Proofs Minted: Unknown
Mint Marks: None
Designer: James Longacre

15. Small Cent (Indian Head) 1860–1864

Size: 19 mm
Weight: 4.67 grams
Edge: Plain
Composition: 88% Copper
                     12% Nickel
Amount Minted: 122,321,000
Proofs Minted: 3,310
Mint Marks: None
Designer: James Longacre

16. Small Cent (Indian Head) 1864–1909

Size: 19 mm
Weight: 3.11 grams
Edge: Plain
Composition: 95% Copper
                     5% Tin/Zinc
Amount Minted: 1,690,916,000
Proofs Minted: 96,848
Mint Marks: S (1908–9)
Designer: James Longacre

17. Small Cent (Lincoln Head) 1909–1942, 1944–1958

Size: 19 mm
Weight 3.11 grams
Edge: Plain
Composition: 95% Copper
        5% Tin/Zinc
Amount Minted: 24,663,560,620
Proofs Minted: 3,851,768
Mint Marks: D and S
Designer: Victor D. Brenner

18. Small Cent (Lincoln Head) 1943

Size: 19 mm
Weight: 2.70 grams
Edge: Plain
Composition: Zinc Coated Steel
Amount Minted: 1,093,838,670
Proofs Minted: None
Mint Marks: D and S
Designer: Victor D. Brenner

19. Small Cent (Lincoln Head-Memorial) 1959–Present

Size: 19 mm
Weight: 3.11 grams
Edge: Plain
Composition: 95% Copper
        5% Tin/Zinc
(1962 to date 5% Zinc)
Mint Marks: D and S
Designers: Victor D. Brenner
        Frank Gasparro

20. Two Cent Piece 1864–1873

Size: 23 mm
Weight: 6.22 grams
Edge: Plain
Composition: 95% Copper
        5% Tin/Zinc
Amount Minted: 45,601,000
Proofs Minted: 1,100
Mint Marks: None
Designer: James Longacre

21. Three Cent Piece (Liberty Head) 1865–1889

Size: 17.9 mm
Weight: 1.94 grams
Edge: Plain
Composition: 75% Copper
            25% Nickel
Amount Minted: 32,378,316
Proofs Minted: 46,889
Mint Marks: None
Designer: James Longacre

22. Three Cent Piece (Single-Line Star) 1851–1853

Size: 14 mm
Weight: .8 gram
Edge: Plain
Composition: 90% Silver
            10% Copper
Amount Minted: 36,230,090
Proofs Minted: None
Mint Marks: O (1851)
Designer: James Longacre

23. Three Cent Piece (Triple-Line Star) 1854–1858

Size: 14 mm
Weight: .75 gram
Edge: Plain
Composition: 90% Silver
            10% Copper
Amount Minted: 4,914,000
Proofs Minted: None Recorded
Mint Marks: None
Designer: James Longacre

24. Three Cent Piece (Double-Line Star) 1859–1873

Size: 14 mm
Weight: .75 gram
Edge: Plain
Composition: 90% Silver
            10% Copper
Amount Minted: 1,581,490
Proofs Minted: 10,840
Mint Marks: None
Designer: James Longacre

155

25. Five Cent (Shield with Rays) 1866–1867

Size: 20.5 mm
Weight: 5.0 grams
Edge: Plain
Composition: 75% Copper
                 25% Nickel
Amount Minted: 14,950,000 approx.
Proofs Minted: Record Incomplete
Mint Marks: None
Designer: James Longacre

26. Five Cent (Shield without Rays) 1867–1883

Size: 20.5 mm
Weight: 5.0 grams
Edge: Plain
Composition: 75% Copper
                 25% Nickel
Amount Minted: 111,413,949
Proofs Minted: 23,099
Mint Marks: None
Designer: James Longacre

27. Five Cent (Liberty Head without "Cents") 1883

Size: 21.2 mm
Weight: 5.0 grams
Edge: Plain
Composition: 75% Copper
                 25% Nickel
Amount Minted: 5,479,519
Proofs Minted: 5,219
Mint Marks: None
Designer: Charles Barber

28. Five Cent (Liberty Head) 1883–1912 (1913)

Size: 21.2 mm
Weight: 5.0 grams
Edge: Plain
Composition: 75% Copper
                 25% Nickel
Amount Minted: 99,197,920
Proofs Minted: 79,921
Mint Marks: S and D (1912)
Designer: Charles Barber

29. Five Cent (Indian Head-Buffalo on Mound) 1913

Size: 21.2 mm
Weight: 5.0 grams
Edge: Plain
Composition: 75% Copper
　　　　　　 25% Nickel
Amount Minted: 38,435,520
Proofs Minted: 1,520
Mint Marks: D and S
Designer: James E. Fraser

30. Five Cent (Indian Head-Buffalo on Plain) 1913–1938

Size: 21.2 mm
Weight: 5.0 grams
Edge: Plain
Composition: 75% Copper
　　　　　　 25% Nickel
Amount Minted: 1,174,084,709
Proofs Minted: 13,114
Mint Marks: D and S
Designer: James E. Fraser

31. Five Cent (Jefferson Head) 1938–1942, 1946–Present

Size: 21.2 mm
Weight: 5.0 grams
Edge: Plain
Composition: 75% Copper
　　　　　　 25% Nickel
Mint Marks: D and S
Designer: Felix Schlag

32. Five Cent (Jefferson Head-WWII Emergency) 1942–1945

Size: 21.2 mm
Weight: 5.0 grams
Edge: Plain
Composition: 56% Copper
　　35% Silver, 9% Manganese
Amount Minted: 869,923,700
Proofs Minted: 27,000 (1942)
Mint Marks: P, D, and S
Designer: Felix Schlag

157

33. Half-Dime (Flowing Hair) 1794–1795

Size: 16.5 mm
Weight: 1.35 grams
Edge: Milled
Composition: 89.2% Silver
                10.8% Copper
Amount Minted: 86,416
Proofs Minted: None Recorded
Mint Marks: None
Designer: Robert Scot

34. Half-Dime (Draped Bust-Small Eagle) 1796–1797

Size: 16.5 mm
Weight: 1.35 grams
Edge: Reeded
Composition: 89.2% Silver
                10.8% Copper
Amount Minted: 54,757
Proofs Minted: None Recorded
Mint Marks: None
Designer: Gilbert Stuart

35. Half-Dime (Draped Bust-Heraldic Eagle) 1800–1805

Size: 16.5 mm
Weight: 1.35 grams
Edge: Reeded
Composition: 90% Silver
              10% Copper
Amount Minted: 124,370
Proofs Minted: None Recorded
Mint Marks: None
Designers: Robert Scot, Gilbert Stuart

36. Half-Dime (Liberty Cap) 1829–1837

Size: 15.5 mm
Weight: 1.35 grams
Edge: Reeded
Composition: 90% Silver
              10% Copper
Amount Minted: 14,463,700
Proofs Minted: None Recorded
Mint Marks: None
Designer: John Reich

158

37. Half-Dime (Liberty Seated-No Stars) 1837–1838

Size: 15.5 mm
Weight: 1.34 grams
Edge: Reeded
Composition: 90% Silver
           10% Copper
Amount Minted: 2,255,000
Proofs Minted: None Recorded
Mint Marks: 0 (1838)
Designer: Christian Gobrecht

38. Half-Dime (Liberty Seated) 1838–1860

Size: 15.5 mm
Weight: 1.34 grams
        1.24 grams
Edge: Reeded
Composition: 90% Silver
           10% Copper
Amount Minted: 20,700,000
    (w/Arrows): 22,860,020
Proofs Minted: None Recorded
Mint Marks: 0
Designer: Christian Gobrecht

Without Drapery

With Drapery

39. Half-Dime (Liberty Seated-without Motto) 1859–1860

Size: 15.5 mm
Weight: 1.24 grams
Edge: Reeded
Composition: 90% Silver
           10% Copper
Amount Minted: 100
Proofs Minted: None Recorded
Mint Marks: None
Designer: Christian Gobrecht

Same design as No. 37 but without motto.

159

40. Half-Dime (Liberty Seated-with Motto) 1860–1873

Size: 15.5 mm
Weight: 1.24 grams
Edge: Reeded
Composition: 90% Silver
          10% Copper
Amount Minted: 15,563,240
Proofs Minted: 10,040
Mint Marks: S and O
Designer: Christian Gobrecht

41. Dime (Draped Bust-Small Eagle) 1796–1797

Size: 19 mm
Weight: 2.70 grams
Edge: Reeded
Composition: 89.2% Silver
          10.8% Copper
Amount Minted: 47,396
Proofs Minted: None Recorded
Mint Marks: None
Designer: Robert Scot

42. Dime (Draped Bust-Heraldic Eagle) 1798–1807

Size: 19 mm
Weight: 2.70 grams
Edge: Reeded
Composition: 89.2% Silver
          10.8% Copper
Amount Minted: 422,010
Proofs Minted: None Recorded
Mint Marks: None
Designer: Robert Scot

43. Dime (Liberty Cap) 1809–1837

Size: 18.8 mm
Weight: 2.70 grams
Edge: Reeded
Composition: 89.2% Silver
          10.8% Copper
Amount Minted: 12,386,329
Proofs Minted: None Recorded
Mint Marks: None
Designers: John Reich
          Robert Scot

44. *Dime (Seated Liberty-No Stars) 1837–1838*

Size: 17.9 mm
Weight: 2.67 grams
Edge: Reeded
Composition: 90% Silver
          10% Copper
Amount Minted: 402,434
Proofs Minted: None Recorded
Mint Marks: O
Designer: Christian Gobrecht

45. *Dime (Seated Liberty-with Stars) 1838–1860*

Size: 17.9 mm
Weight: 2.67 grams in 1838
         2.49 grams in 1853–60
Edge: Reeded
Composition: 90% Silver
          10% Copper
Amount Minted: 72,820,744
Proofs Minted: Rare
Mint Marks: O and S
Designer: Christian Gobrecht

46. *Dime (The Christian Gobrecht Liberty Seated) 1859*

Size: 17.9 mm
Weight: 2.49 grams
Edge: Reeded
Composition: 90% Silver
          10% Copper
Amount Minted: Unavailable
Proofs Minted: None
Mint Marks: None
Designer: Christian Gobrecht

Same design as No. 44 but struck without "United States of America."

47. *Dime (Liberty Seated-with Motto) 1860–1891*

Size: 17.9 mm
Weight: 2.49 grams in 1860
         2.50 grams in 1873–91
Edge: Reeded
Composition: 90% Silver
          10% Copper
Amount Minted: 181,959,408
Proofs Minted: 46,803
Mint Marks: O, S, and CC
Designer: Christian Gobrecht

161

48. Dime (Liberty Head) 1892–1916

Size: 17.9 mm
Weight: 2.50 grams
Edge: Reeded
Composition: 90% Silver
              10% Copper
Amount Minted: 503,263,328
Proofs Minted: 17,343
Mint Marks: O, S, and D
Designer: Charles Barber

49. Dime (Winged Liberty-"Mercury") 1916–1945

Size: 17.9 mm
Weight: 2.50 grams
Edge: Reeded
Composition: 90% Silver
              10% Copper
Amount Minted: 2,677,941,528
Proofs Minted: 78,648
Mint Marks: D and S
Designer: A. A. Weinman

50. Dime (Roosevelt Head) 1946–1964

Size: 17.9 mm
Weight: 2.50 grams
Edge: Reeded
Composition: 90% Silver
              10% Copper
Amount Minted: 5,161,379,795
Proofs Minted: 19,837,717
Mint Marks: D and S
Designer: John Sinnock

51. Dime (Roosevelt Head) 1965–Present

Size: 17.9 mm
Weight: 2.27 grams
Edge: Reeded
Composition: 75% Copper
              25% Nickel
Mint Marks: D and S
Designer: John Sinnock

52. Twenty Cent (Liberty Seated) 1875–1878

Size: 22 mm
Weight: 50 grams
Edge: Plain
Composition: 90% Silver
           10% Copper
Amount Minted: 1,355,000
Proofs Minted: 3,460
Mint Marks: S and CC
Designer: Christian Gobrecht

53. Quarter Dollar (Draped Bust) 1796

Size: 27.5 mm
Weight: 6.74 grams
Edge: Reeded
Composition: 89.2% Silver
           10.8% Copper
Amount Minted: 6,146
Proofs Minted: None Recorded
Mint Marks: None
Designer: Robert Scot

54. Quarter Dollar (Draped Bust-Heraldic Eagle) 1804–1807

Size: 27.5 mm
Weight: 6.74 grams
Edge: Reeded
Composition: 89.2% Silver
           10.8% Copper
Amount Minted: 554,899
Proofs Minted: None Recorded
Mint Marks: None
Designer: John Reich

55. Quarter Dollar (Liberty Cap-with Motto) 1815–1828

Size: 27 mm in 1815
      26.0 mm in 1818–28
Weight: 6.74 grams
Edge: Reeded
Composition: 89.2% Silver
           10.8% Copper
Amount Minted: 1,274,581
Proofs Minted: None Recorded
Mint Marks: None
Designer: John Reich

163

56. *Quarter Dollar (Liberty Cap-without Motto)*
1831–1838

Size: 24.3 mm
Weight: 6.74 grams
Edge: Reeded
Composition: 89.2% Silver
                10.8% Copper
Amount Minted: 4,668,400
Proofs Minted: Rare
Mint Marks: None
Designer: William Kneass

57. *Quarter Dollar (Liberty Seated-without Rays)*
1838–1866

Size: 24.3 mm
Weight: 6.68 grams
Edge: Reeded
Composition: 90% Silver
                10% Copper
Amount Minted: 54,016,380
Proofs Minted: 3,920
Mint Marks: O and S
Designer: Christian Gobrecht

58. *Quarter Dollar (Liberty Seated) 1853*

Size: 24.3 mm
Weight: 6.22 grams
Edge: Reeded
Composition: 90% Silver
                10% Copper
Amount Minted: 16,586,220
Proofs Minted: Rare
Mint Marks: O
Designer: Christian Gobrecht

59. *Quarter Dollar (Liberty Seated-without Motto)* *1866–1891*

Size: 24.3 mm
Weight: 6.68 grams in 1866–73
6.25 grams in 1873–91
Edge: Reeded
Composition: 90% Silver
10% Copper
Amount Minted: 75,014,816
Proofs Minted: 21,313
Mint Marks: O, S, D, and CC
Designer: Christian Gobrecht

60. *Quarter Dollar (Liberty Head) 1892–1916*

Size: 24.3 mm
Weight: 6.25 grams
Edge: Reeded
Composition: 90% Silver
10% Copper
Amount Minted: 264,286,491
Proofs Minted: 17,299
Mint Marks: O, S, and D
Designer: Charles Barber

61. *Quarter Dollar (Standing Liberty) 1916–1917*

Size: 24.3 mm
Weight: 6.25 grams
Edge: Reeded
Composition: 90% Silver
10% Copper
Amount Minted: 12,305,200
Proofs Minted: None Recorded
Mint Marks: D and S
Designer: Hermon MacNeil

Full Head Detail

Bare Breast
1916-1917

165

62. Quarter Dollar (Standing Liberty-with Vest) 1917–1930

Size: 24.3 mm
Weight: 6.25 grams
Edge: Reeded
Composition: 90% Silver
          10% Copper
Amount Minted: 215,516,800
Proofs Minted: None Recorded
Mint Marks: D and S
Designer: Hermon MacNeil

Normal Head Detail

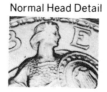

63. Quarter Dollar (Washington Head-Silver) 1932–1964

Size: 24.3 mm
Weight: 6.25 grams
Edge: Reeded
Composition: 90% Silver
          10% Copper
Amount Minted: 2,044,710,652
Proofs Minted: 19,905,612
Mint Marks: D and S
Designer: John Flanagan

64. Quarter Dollar (Washington Head-Clad) 1965–Present

Size: 24.3 mm
Weight: 5.67 grams
Edge: Reeded
Composition: 75% Copper
          25% Nickel
Mint Marks: D and S
Designer: John Flanagan

65. Half Dollar (Flowing Hair) 1794–1795

Size: 32.5 mm
Weight: 13.48 grams
Edge: Lettered
Composition: 89.2% Silver
            10.8% Copper
Amount Minted: 323,144
Proofs Minted: None Recorded
Mint Marks: None
Designer: Robert Scot or
          John Gardner

66. Half Dollar (Draped Bust-Small Eagle) 1796–1797

Size: 32.5 mm
Weight: 13.48 grams
Edge: Lettered
Composition: 89.2% Silver
            10.8% Copper
Amount Minted: 3,918
Proofs Minted: None Recorded
Mint Marks: None
Designer: Robert Scot

67. Half Dollar (Draped Bust-Heraldic Eagle) 1801–1806

Size: 32.5 mm
Weight: 13.48 grams
Edge: Lettered
Composition: 89.2% Silver
            10.8% Copper
Amount Minted: 1,444,268
Proofs Minted: None Recorded
Mint Marks: None
Designer: Robert Scot

167

68. Half Dollar (Liberty Capped-with Motto) 1807–1836

Size: 32.5 mm
Weight: 13.48 grams
Edge: Lettered to 1836
　　　Reeded 1836
Composition: 89.2% Silver
　　　　　　10.8% Copper
Amount Minted: 82,293,204
Proofs Minted: None Recorded
Mint Marks: None
Designer: John Reich

69. Half Dollar (Liberty Capped-without Motto) 1836–1837

Size: 30 mm
Weight: 13.48 grams in 1836
　　　　13.36 grams in 1837
Edge: Reeded
Composition: 89.2%, 10.8% (1836)
　　　　　　90%, 10% (1837)
Amount Minted: 3,629,820
Proofs Minted: Rare
Mint Marks: None
Designer: Christian Gobrecht

70. Half Dollar (Liberty Cap) 1838–1839

Size: 30 mm
Weight: 13.36 grams
Edge: Reeded
Composition: 90% Silver
　　　　　　10% Copper
Amount Minted: 7,043,556
Proofs Minted: Rare
Mint Marks: 0
Designer: Christian Gobrecht

71. Half Dollar (Liberty Seated-without Rays) 1839–1866

Size: 30.6 mm
Weight: 13.36 grams (1839–53)
        12.44 grams (1853–66)
Edge: Reeded
Composition: 90% Silver
        10% Copper
Amount Minted: 90,326,651
Proofs Minted: 2,980
Mint Marks: O and S
Designer: Christian Gobrecht

72. Half Dollar (Liberty Seated-with Rays) 1853

Size: 30.6 mm
Weight: 12.44 grams
Edge: Reeded
Composition: 90% Silver
        10% Copper
Amount Minted: 4,960,708
Proofs Minted: None
Mint Marks: O
Designer: Christian Gobrecht

73. Half Dollar (Liberty Seated-with Motto) 1866–1891

Size: 30.6 mm
Weight: 12.44 grams (1866–72)
        12.50 grams (1873–91)
Edge: Reeded
Composition: 90% Silver
        10% Copper
Amount Minted: 61,395,551
Proofs Minted: 20,873
Mint Marks: S and CC
Designer: Christian Gobrecht

74. Half Dollar (Liberty Head) 1892–1915

Size: 30.6 mm
Weight: 12.50 grams
Edge: Reeded
Composition: 90% Silver
              10% Copper
Amount Minted: 142,843,922
Proofs Minted: 17,313
Mint Marks: O, S, and D
Designer: Charles Barber

75. Half Dollar (Walking Liberty) 1916–1947

Size: 30.6 mm
Weight: 12.50 grams
Edge: Reeded
Composition: 90% Silver
              10% Copper
Amount Minted: 485,478,441
Proofs Minted: 74,400
Mint Marks: D and S
Designer: Adolph Weinman

76. Half Dollar (Franklin Head) 1948–1963

Size: 30.6 mm
Weight: 12.50 grams
Edge: Reeded
Composition: 90% Silver
              10% Copper
Amount Minted: 481,801,407
Proofs Minted: 15,886,955
Mint Marks: D and S
Designer: John Sinnock

77. Half Dollar (Kennedy Head-Silver) 1964

Size: 30.6 mm
Weight: 12.50 grams
Edge: Reeded
Composition: 90% Silver
                10% Copper
Amount Minted: 433,460,212
Proofs Minted: 3,950,762
Mint Marks: D
Designers: Gilroy Roberts
             Frank Gasparro

78. Half Dollar (Kennedy Head-Clad) 1965–1970

Size: 30.6 mm
Weight: 11.50 grams
Edge: Reeded
Composition:
   Core: 40% Silver, 60% Copper
   Clad: 80% Silver, 20% Copper
Amount Minted: 553,850,972
Proofs Minted: 8,608,947
Mint Marks: D and S
Designers: Gilroy Roberts, Frank Gasparro

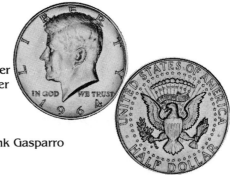

79. One Dollar (Flowing Hair) 1794–1795

Size: 39.5 mm
Weight: 26.96 grams
Edge: Lettered
Composition: 89.2% Silver
                10.8% Copper
Amount Minted: 204,791
Proofs Minted: Questionable
Mint Marks: None
Designers: Robert Scot
             John Gardner

80. *One Dollar (Draped Bust-Small Eagle) 1795–1798*

Size: 39.5 mm
Weight: 26.96 grams
Edge: Lettered
Composition: 89.2% Silver
　　　　　　　10.8% Copper
Amount Minted: 403,322
Proofs Minted: None Recorded
Mint Marks: None
Designer: Gilbert Stuart

81. *One Dollar (Draped Bust-Heraldic Eagle) 1798–1803*

Size: 39.5 mm
Weight: 26.96 grams
Edge: Lettered
Composition: 89.2% Silver
　　　　　　　10.8% Copper
Amount Minted: 806,603
Proofs Minted: Rare
Mint Marks: None
Designer: Gilbert Stuart

172

82. The 1804 Silver Dollar (Same Pattern as 1803)

This is the most mysterious and scarcest piece in United States coinage. Officially, there are no dollars with this date. Those bearing the date 1804 are from two possible points of origin—inside or outside the United States Mint. The few struck with mint facilities have been verified as post-dated pieces (made after 1804).

83. One Dollar (The Christian Gobrecht Dollar) 1836

Size: Specimen Dollar
Weight: Unavailable
Edge: Plain and Reeded
Composition: 90% Silver
                10% Copper
Amount Minted: 1,026
Proofs Minted: 1,026
Mint Marks: None
Designer: Christian Gobrecht

84. One Dollar (Liberty Seated-without Motto) 1840–1866

Size: 38.1 mm
Weight: 26.73 grams
Edge: Reeded
Composition: 90% Silver
           10% Copper
Amount Minted: 2,895,673
Proofs Minted: 4,390
Mint Marks: O and S
Designers: Christian Gobrecht
         Robert Hughes

85. One Dollar (Liberty Seated-with Motto) 1866–1873

Size: 38.1 mm
Weight: 26.73 grams
Edge: Reeded
Composition: 90% Silver
           10% Copper
Amount Minted: 3,603,948
Proofs Minted: 6,060
Mint Marks: S and CC
Designers: Christian Gobrecht
         Robert Hughes

174

86. One Dollar (Trade Dollar-Liberty Seated) 1873–1885

Size: 38.1 mm
Weight: 27.22 grams
Edge: Reeded
Composition: 90% Silver
              10%Copper
Amount Minted: 35,960,360
Proofs Minted: 11,404
Mint Marks: S and CC
Designer: William Barber

87. One Dollar (Liberty Head-Morgan) 1878–1904, 1921

Size: 38.1 mm
Weight: 26.73 grams
Edge: Reeded
Composition: 90% Silver
              10% Copper
Amount Minted: 627,451,520
Proofs Minted: 23,416
Mint Marks: O, D, S, and CC
Designer: George Morgan

88. One Dollar (Liberty Head-Peace) 1921–1935

Size: 38.1 mm
Weight: 26.73 grams
Edge: Reeded
Composition: 90% Silver
            10% Copper
Amount Minted: 190,577,270
Proofs Minted: None Recorded
Mint Marks: D and S
Designer: Anthony DeFrancisci

89. One Dollar (Eisenhower Head-Silver Clad) 1971–1974

Size: 38.1 mm
Weight: 24.59 grams
Edge: Reeded
Composition: 40.9% Silver
            59.1% Copper
Amount Minted: 374,521,000
Proofs Minted: 8,405,119
Mint Marks: S and D
Designer: Frank Gasparro

90. One Dollar (Eisenhower Head-Bicentennial) 1976

Size: 38.1 mm
Weight: Silver Issue: 24.59 grams
        Clad Issue: 22.63 grams
Edge: Reeded
Composition: Silver Issue: 50% Silver,
            50% Copper
            Clad Issue: 75% Copper,
            25% Nickel
Amount Minted: 242,559,180
Proofs Minted: 10,995,180
Mint Marks: D and S
Designer: Frank Gasparro

91. One Dollar (Eisenhower Head-Copper/Nickel) 1977–78

Size: 38.1 mm
Weight: 22.68
Edge: Reeded
Composition: 75% Copper, 25% Nickel
Amount Minted: 100,672,829
Proofs Minted: 6,378,933
Mint Marks: D and S
Designer: Frank Gasparro

Same design as No. 89.

92. One Dollar (Susan B. Anthony) 1979–1981

Size: 26.5 mm
Weight: 8.1 grams
Edge: Reeded
Composition: 75% Copper
            25% Nickel
Amount Minted: Unavailable
Proofs Minted: Unavailable
Mint Marks: D, S
Designer: Frank Gasparro

177

GOLD

93. One Dollar (Liberty Head) 1849–1854

Size: 13 mm
Weight: 1.672 grams
Edge: Reeded
Std. Fineness: 900/1000
Amount Minted: 12,649,120
Proofs Minted: None Recorded
Mint Marks: C, D, O, and S
Designer: James Longacre

94. One Dollar (Indian Head-Female) 1854–1856

Size: 15 mm
Weight: 1.672 grams
Edge: Reeded
Std. Fineness: 900/1000
Amount Minted: 849,487
Proofs Minted: None Recorded
Mint Marks: C, D, S, and O
Designer: James Longacre

95. One Dollar (Large Indian Head-Female) 1856–1889

Size: 15 mm
Weight: 1.672 grams
Edge: Reeded
Std. Fineness: 900/1000
Amount Minted: 5,300,634
Proofs Minted: 8,429
Mint Marks: D, C, and S
Designer: James Longacre

96. Quarter Eagle (Liberty Cap-without Stars) 1796

Size: 20 mm
Weight: 4.37 grams
Edge: Reeded
Std. Fineness: 916.6/1000
Amount Minted: 897 approx.
Proofs Minted: None Recorded
Mint Marks: None
Designer: Robert Scot

178

97. *Quarter Eagle (Liberty Cap-with Stars) 1796–1807*

Size: 20 mm
Weight: 4.37 grams
Edge: Reeded
Std. Fineness: 916.6/1000
Amount Minted: 18,584
Proofs Minted: None Recorded
Mint Marks: None
Designer: Robert Scot

98. *Quarter Eagle (Liberty Cap-Broken Stars) 1808*

Size: 20 mm
Weight: 4.37 grams
Edge: Reeded
Std. Fineness: 916.6/1000
Amount Minted: 2,710
Proofs Minted: None Recorded
Mint Marks: None
Designer: John Reich

99. *Quarter Eagle (Liberty Cap) 1821–1834*

Size: 18.5 mm
Weight: 4.37 grams
Edge: Reeded
Std. Fineness: 916.6/1000
Amount Minted: 46,065
Proofs Minted: None Recorded
Mint Marks: None
Designer: Robert Scot

100. *Quarter Eagle (Classic Head) 1834–1839*

Size: 18.2 mm
Weight: 4.18 grams
Edge: Reeded
Std. Fineness: 899.25/1000
              900/1000 in 1837
Amount Minted: 968,289
Proofs Minted: None
Mint Marks: C, D, and O
Designer: William Kneass

101. Quarter Eagle (Coronet) 1840–1907

Size: 18 mm
Weight: 4.18 grams
Edge: Reeded
Std. Fineness: 900/1000
Amount Minted: 12,200,225
Proofs Minted: 4,047
Mint Marks: C, D, S, and O
Designer: Christian Gobrecht

102. Quarter Eagle (Indian Head) 1908–1929

Size: 18 mm
Weight: 4.18 grams
Edge: Reeded
Std. Fineness: 900/1000
Amount Minted: 7,252,088
Proofs Minted: 1,728
Mint Marks: D
Designer: Bela Lyons Pratt

103. Three Dollars (Indian Head-Female) 1854–1889

Size: 20.5 mm
Weight: 5.015 grams
Edge: Reeded
Std. Fineness: 916.6/1000
Amount Minted: 539,883
Proofs Minted: 1,949
Mint Marks: S, D, and O
Designer: James Longacre

104. Half Eagle (Liberty Cap-Small Eagle) 1795–1796

Size: 25 mm
Weight: 8.75 grams
Edge: Reeded
Std. Fineness: 916.6/1000
Amount Minted: Inaccurate Records
Proofs Minted: None Recorded
Mint Marks: None
Designer: Robert Scot

180

105. Half Eagle (Liberty Cap-Heraldic Eagle) 1795–1807

Size: 25 mm
Weight: 8.75 grams
Edge: Reeded
Std. Fineness: 916.6/1000
Amount Minted: Inaccurate Records
Proofs Minted: None Recorded
Mint Marks: None
Designer: Robert Scot

106. Half Eagle (Liberty Cap-Broken Stars) 1807–1812

Size: 25 mm
Weight: 8.75 grams
Edge: Reeded
Std. Fineness: 916.6/1000
Amount Minted: 1,784,625
Proofs Minted: None Recorded
Mint Marks: None
Designer: John Reich

107. Half Eagle (Liberty Cap) 1813–1834

Size: 26 mm
Weight: 8.75 grams
Edge: Reeded
Std. Fineness: 916.6/1000
Amount Minted: 1,385,612
Proofs Minted: None Recorded
Mint Marks: None
Designer: Robert Scot

108. Half Eagle (Classic Head) 1834–1838

Size: 22.5 mm
Weight: 8.36 grams
Edge: Reeded
Std. Fineness: 899.25/1000
              900/1000 in 1837
Amount Minted: 2,114,180
Proofs Minted: None Recorded
Mint Marks: C and D
Designer: William Kneass

181

109. Half Eagle (Coronet-without Motto) 1839–1866

Size: 21.6 mm
Weight: 8.359 grams
Edge: Reeded
Std. Fineness: 900/1000
Amount Minted: 8,694,434
Proofs Minted: 268
Mint Marks: C, D, S, and O
Designer: Christian Gobrecht

110. Half Eagle (Coronet-with Motto) 1866–1908

Size: 21.6 mm
Weight: 8.359 grams
Edge: Reeded
Std. Fineness: 900/1000
Amount Minted: 47,181,832
Proofs Minted: 2,927
Mint Marks: C, D, S, and O
Designer: Christian Gobrecht

111. Half Eagle (Indian Head) 1908–1929

Size: 21.6 mm
Weight: 8.359 grams
Edge: Reeded
Std. Fineness: 900/1000
Amount Minted: 14,079,242
Proofs Minted: 1,077
Mint Marks: D,O, and S
Designer: Bela Lyons Pratt

112. Eagle (Liberty Cap-Small Eagle) 1795–1797

Size: 33 mm
Weight: 17.5 grams
Edge: Reeded
Std. Fineness: 916.6/1000
Amount Minted: 12,195
Proofs Minted: None Recorded
Mint Marks: None
Designer: Robert Scot

113. Eagle (Liberty Cap-Heraldic Eagle) 1797–1804

Size: 33 mm
Weight: 17.5 grams
Edge: Reeded
Std. Fineness: 916.6/1000
Amount Minted: 108,308
Proofs Minted: None Recorded
Mint Marks: None
Designer: Robert Scot

114. Eagle (Coronet-without Motto) 1837–1866

Size: 27 mm
Weight: 16.718 grams
Edge: Reeded
Std. Fineness: 899.25/1000
              900/1000 in 1837
Amount Minted: 5,394,338
Proofs Minted: 259
Mint Marks: O and S
Designer: Christian Gobrecht

115. Eagle (Coronet-with Motto) 1866–1907

Size: 27 mm
Weight: 16.718 grams
Edge: Reeded
Std. Fineness: 900/1000
Amount Minted: 36,382,594
Proofs Minted: 2,293
Mint Marks: S, CC, O, and D
Designer: Christian Gobrecht

116. Eagle (Indian Head-without Motto) 1907–1908

Size: 27 mm
Weight: 16.718 grams
Edge: Starred (46)
Std. Fineness: 900/1000
Amount Minted: 483,448
Proofs Minted: None Recorded
Mint Marks: D
Designer: Augustus Saint-Gaudens

117. Eagle (Indian Head-with Motto) 1908–1933

Size: 27 mm
Weight: 16.718 grams
Edge: Starred (46 to 1912)
          (48 thereafter)
Std. Fineness: 900/1000
Amount Minted: 14,385,907
Proofs Minted: 768
Mint Marks: D and S
Designer: Augustus Saint-Gaudens

118. Double Eagle (Coronet-without Motto) 1849–1866

Size: 34 mm
Weight: 33.46 grams
Edge: Reeded
Std. Fineness: 900/1000
Amount Minted: 23,514,279
Proofs Minted: 140
Mint Marks: O and S
Designer: James Longacre

119. Double Eagle (Coronet-with Motto) 1866–1876

Size: 34 mm
Weight: 33.46 grams
Edge: Reeded
Std. Fineness: 900/1000
Amount Minted: 16,161,143
Proofs Minted: 335
Mint Marks: CC and S
Designer: James Longacre

120. Double Eagle (Coronet) 1877–1907

Size: 34 mm
Weight: 33.46 grams
Edge: Reeded
Std. Fineness: 900/1000
Amount Minted: 64,429,851
Proofs Minted: 2,311
Mint Marks: CC, S, O, and D
Designer: James Longacre

121. Double Eagle (Standing Liberty-Roman Numerals) 1907

Size: 34 mm
Weight: 33.46 grams
Edge: Wire Rim
Std. Fineness: 900/1000
Amount Minted: 11,256
Proofs Minted: None
Mint Marks: None
Designer: Augustus Saint-Gaudens

122. Double Eagle (Standing Liberty-Arabic Numerals) 1907–8

Size: 34 mm
Weight: 33.46 grams
Edge: Starred and Lettered
Std. Fineness: 900/1000
Amount Minted: 5,296,968
Proofs Minted: None
Mint Marks: D
Designer: Augustus Saint-Gaudens

123. Double Eagle (Standing Liberty-with Motto) 1908–1933

Size: 34 mm
Weight: 33.46 grams
Edge: Starred
Std. Fineness: 900/1000
Amount Minted: 64,536,365
Proofs Minted: 687
Mint Marks: D and S
Designer: Augustus Saint-Gaudens

Appendix

II

U.S. MUSEUMS EXHIBITING RARE COINS AND RARE CURRENCIES

California

Los Angeles. Los Angeles Airport, Airport-Century branch of the United California Bank, 9841 Airport Blvd. Coins, medals, bank notes, first-day covers, and paper money. Open during regular banking hours.

San Francisco. Bank of California Money Museum, 400 California St. Gold, coins, ingots, bullion, fiscal paper, currency, and early bank drafts. Open 9–3:30 Monday through Thursday, 9–5 Friday, closed national holidays.

San Francisco. The Bank of California's Museum, 400 California St. Special exhibit, "Money of the American West," featuring pioneer gold coins, bars, nuggets, paper money. Open to public 10–3 Monday through Thursday, 3–5 Friday, closed weekends and bankers' holidays.

San Francisco. Old Mint Museum, 5th and Mission Sts. Coins, medals, tokens, paper money, million dollars in gold bullion, antiques, other related items. Open to the public 10–4 Tuesday through Sunday, closed Thanksgiving, Christmas, New Year's Day. Free.

San Francisco. Wells Fargo Bank's History Room, 420 Montgomery St. Gold bars, coins, medals. Open to public 10–3 Monday through Friday, closed weekends and bankers' holidays.

Colorado

Colorado Springs. American Numismatic Association, 818 N. Cascade Ave. Broad scope of coins, medals, tokens, paper money, and a numismatic library. Open to public 10–5 Monday through Friday, closed national holidays. Free.

Colorado Springs. Pioneers' Museum, 25 W. Kiowa St. Coins, medals, paper money. Open to public 10–5 Tuesday through Saturday, 2–5 Sunday, closed national holidays. Free.

Denver. The Denver Art Museum, 11 W. 14th Ave. Parkway. Early Greek coins. Open to public 9–5 Tuesday through Saturday, 9–9 Wednesday, 1–5 Sunday, open for study by appointment only. Closed all national holidays. Free.

Fort Collins. Pioneer Museum, 219 Peterson St. Coins, medals, tokens, paper money. Open to public 1–5 Monday through Saturday, closed national holidays. Accepts donations.

188

Connecticut

Hartford. Connecticut State Library Museum, 231 Capitol Ave. Coins, medals, tokens, paper money, numismatic literature. Open to public 9–5 Monday through Friday, 9–1 Saturday, closed national holidays. Free.

Mystic. G. W. Blunt White Library, The Marine Historical Association. Paper money. Open to public 9–5 Monday through Friday, closed Christmas and New Year's Day.

Mystic. Mystic Seaport, Inc. Coins and medals. Available to scholars upon written application because most are in storage. Museum open 9–5 Monday through Sunday, 10–5 off season, closed Christmas and New Year's Day.

Delaware

Dover. Delaware State Museum, 316 S. Governors Ave. Coins, medals, tokens, paper money on short-term exhibit. Open to public 10–5 Tuesday through Saturday, 1–5 Sunday, closed national holidays. Free.

District of Columbia

Washington. B'Nai B'Rith Museum, 1640 Rhode Island Ave., N.W. Coins and medals of Israel. Open to public 9–5 Sunday through Friday, closed national holidays. Free.

Washington. Corcoran Gallery of Art, 17th and E Sts., N.W. Medals, available by appointment only. Museum open 11–5 Tuesday through Sunday, closed national holidays. Free Tuesday and Wednesday, $1 Thursday through Sunday.

Washington. Daughters of the American Revolution Museum, 1776 D St., N.W. Medals and paper money. Open to public by prior arrangement for stored items. Open 9–4 Monday through Friday, closed national holidays and the week of April 19. Free.

Washington. Smithsonian Institution, Museum of History and Technology, United States National Museum, Constitution Ave. at 14th St., N.W. on the Mall. The most extensive numismatic display in the United States. Coins, medals, tokens, and paper money. Open to public 10–5:30 Monday through Sunday, closed Christmas Day. Free.

Washington. Smithsonian Institution, National Collection of Fine Arts, Constitution Ave. at 10th St., N.W., galleries in the Museum of Natural History Building. Coins and medals available by appointment only. Museum open 10–5:30 Monday through Sunday, closed national holidays. Free.

Washington. U.S. Treasury, east of White House, 15th and Pennsylvania Ave., N.W., first floor. Displays, products of Mint; activities under jurisdiction of the Treasury. Open 8:30–3:30 Tuesday through Friday, 10–12 Saturday, closed Monday, Sunday, and national holidays.

Florida

Fort Pierce. St. Lucie Museum, Pepper State Park. Coins, Spanish treasure. Open to public 9–5 Wednesday through Sunday. Fifty cents admission.

Plantation Key. McKee's Sunken Treasury Fortress, Treasure Harbor, Florida Keys. Coins, medals, tokens, silver bars. Open to public 9–5 every day. $2.50 for adults.

Georgia

Dahlonega. Dahlonega Courthouse Gold Museum. Coins. Open to public 9–5 Tuesday through Saturday, 2–5:30 Sunday, closed Christmas and Thanksgiving. Free.

Dahlonega. North Georgia College. A complete set of gold coins minted at the Dahlonega Branch Mint. Open to public 8–5 Monday through Friday, closed Thanksgiving and Christmas. Free.

Illinois

Chicago. Balzekas Museum of Lithuanian Culture, 4012 Archer Ave. Coins, medals, tokens, paper money, numismatic literature. Open to scholars and to the public 1–4:30 Monday through Sunday. Free.

Chicago. Polish National Alliance, 1201 W. Division St. Coins and medals. Open to scholars and to the public 9–4:45 Monday through Sunday, closed national holidays. Free.

Urbana. World Heritage Museum, University of Illinois at Urbana-Champaign, 484 Lincoln Hall. Extensive collection of ancient and other coins and medals, primitive currency. Ancient coins open to scholars only. Open to public 9–5 Monday through Friday, 9–12 Saturday, 2–5 Sunday. Open when university classes are in session. Free.

Indiana

Evansville. Evansville Museum of Arts and Sciences, 411 S.E. Riverside Dr. Coins, medals, tokens, paper money, numismatic literature, ingots. Open to scholars only. Museum open 10–5 Tuesday through Saturday, 12–5 Sunday, closed Monday, national holidays, at noon on December 24 and 31. Free.

Fort Wayne. Lincoln Museum, 1301 S. Harrison St. Coins, medals, and paper money. Lincolniana. Open to public 8–4:30 Monday through Thursday, 8–12:30 Friday, closed national holidays, Friday after Thanksgiving. Free.

Indianapolis. U.S. Army Finance Corps Museum, in the U.S. Army Finance and Accounting Center, Ft. Benjamin Harrison. Military Payment Certificates, Allied Military Currency, payrolls, expenditure vouchers; also mementos of foreign countries. Open to public 8–4 Monday through Friday, closed national holidays. Free.

Peru. Puterbaugh Museum, 11 N. Huntington St. Coins, tokens, paper money, bonds, numismatic literature. Open to public 1–5 daily except Wednesdays and Sundays, closed national holidays. Free.

Kansas

Baldwin. Old Castle Museum, Baker University. Coins, medals, tokens, paper money. Open to public 2–5 daily except Monday, closed Christmas and New Year's Day. Free, donations accepted.

Louisiana

Shreveport. The R. W. Norton Art Gallery, 4700 block of Creswell Ave. Coins, medals, tokens, paper money, and numismatic literature. Open to public 1–5 daily except Mondays, closed national holidays. Free.

Maine

York. Wilcox House. Paper money. Open to public 9:30–5 Monday through Saturday, 1:30–5 Sunday. Closed June 15 to Sept. 30. $1 for adults, $.25 for children.

Massachusetts

Boston. New Federal Reserve Bank of Boston, Federal Reserve Plaza. Houses a money museum of ancient, European, and early American coins and paper money.

Lynn. Lynn Historical Society, 125 Green St. Coins, medals, tokens, paper money. Open to scholars only 9–12 Monday through Friday, closed national holidays.

Salem. Peabody Museum of Salem, 161 Essex St. Coins, medals, tokens, paper money. Stored items open to scholars only. Open to public 9–5 Monday through Saturday, 1–5 Sunday, closed Christmas and New Year's Day. $1 for adults, $.50 for children.

Worcester. American Antiquarian Society, Salisbury St. and Park Ave. Medals, paper money, numismatic literature. Open to scholars only. Museum open 9–5 Monday through Friday, closed national holidays. Free

Michigan

Ann Arbor. William L. Clements Library, University of Michigan. Paper money available to scholars only. Library open 9–5 Monday through Friday, closed national holidays. Free.

Detroit. Detroit Historical Museum, 5401 Woodward Ave. Coins, medals, paper money. Available to scholars only. Museum open 9–5 Tuesday through Saturday, 1–5 Sunday. Free.

Detroit. Museum of Money, National Bank of Detroit, Woodward and Fort Sts. Extensive collection of coins, medals, tokens, paper money, numismatic literature, and other related items. Open to public 9–5 Monday through Friday, closed national holidays. Free.

Missouri

Columbia. Museum of Art and Archeology, University of Missouri. Ancient and modern coins, medals, tokens, paper money. Extensive collection of numismatic literature. Open to public 2–5 daily, closed national holidays. Free.

Independence. Truman Library. Coins, medals, paper money. Open to public 8:30–5 daily, closed Christmas, Thanksgiving, New Year's Day. $.50 admission.

Point Lookout. John Paul Butler Collection of Monies of the World, Ralph Foster Museum, the School of the Ozarks. Large collection of coins, medals, tokens, paper money, numismatic literature, and other related items. Open to public 8–5 Monday through Saturday, 1–5 Sunday, closed Christmas and New Year's Day. Free.

St. Louis. Concordia Historical Institute, 801 De Mun Ave. Coins, medals, tokens, paper money, numismatic literature. Open to public 8–5 Monday through Friday, 2–5 weekends, closed national holidays. Free.

Montana

Virginia City. Virginia City-Madison County Historical Museum. Coins, tokens, paper money. Open to public 8–8 daily June to September 15. Free.

Nebraska

Boys Town. Philamatic Center. Coins, medals, tokens, paper money, numismatic literature, other related items. Open to public 8–4 Monday through Friday, 9–4 Sunday, closed Christmas, New Year's Day, Thanksgiving. Free.

Lincoln. Division of Numismatics and Philatelics, University of Nebraska State Museum, W436 Nebraska Hall. Coins, medals, tokens, paper money, numismatic literature, other related items. Open to scholars only, by appointment. Free.

Omaha. Joslyn Art Museum, 2200 Dodge St. Coins, medals, tokens, paper money. Open to scholars by appointment, some open to the public 10–5 Tuesday through Friday, closed national holidays. Free.

Omaha. Omaha Public Library. Large collection of numismatic literature. Open to public 9–5:30 Monday through Saturday, closed national holidays. Free.

New Hampshire

Hanover. Dartmouth College Museum. Coins, paper money, numismatic literature in the Baker Library. Open to public 9–5 Monday through Saturday, 2–5 Sunday, closed Christmas. Free.

Manchester. The Manchester Historic Association, 129 Amherst St. Medals, tokens, paper money. Open to public on request, 9–4 Tuesday through Friday, 10–4 Saturday, closed national holidays. Free.

New Jersey

Newark. The New Jersey Historical Society, 230 Broadway Ave. Coins, medals, tokens, paper money. Presently unavailable for viewing.

Newark. The Newark Museum, 49 Washington St. Extensive collection of coins, medals, tokens, paper money, numismatic literature, and other related items. Some in storage and available by appointment only. Open to public 12–5 Monday through Saturday, 1–5 Sunday and holidays. Closed New Year's Day, July 4, Thanksgiving, Christmas. Free.

Paterson. Passaic County Historical Society, Lambert Castle, Garret Mountain Reservation. Coins, medals, tokens, paper money, available to scholars only. Museum open 1–4:45 Wednesday through Friday, 11–4:45 Saturday and Sunday. Closed Thanksgiving and Dec. 25–Jan. 1. Free.

Princeton. The Art Museum, Princeton University. Greek and Roman coins. Italian, Renaissance, and modern medals. Open to scholars only by appointment. Museum open 10–4 Monday through Friday, closed national holidays. Free.

New York

Buffalo. Buffalo and Erie County Historical Society, 25 Nottingham Court. Coins, medals, tokens, paper money, numismatic literature. Presently no facilities for first-hand viewing, photo catalogs available. Open 9–5 Monday through Friday, closed national holidays. Free.

Hyde Park. Franklin Roosevelt Library Museum. Coins, medals, tokens, paper money, numismatic literature, other related items. Available to scholars only. Museum open 9–5 Monday through Friday, closed Christmas. No cost for research.

Ithaca. Dewitt Historical Society Museum. Coins, medals, tokens, other related items. Some available to scholars only. Open to public 12:30–5 Tuesday through Saturday, closed national holidays. Free.

New York. The American Numismatic Society, Broadway between 155th and 156th Sts. The most extensive numismatic collection in the United States, including over a million items: coins, medals, decorations, paper money, numismatic literature. Selections from the collection are on display for the public and ANS members, 9–5 Tuesday through Saturday, 1–4 Sunday, closed national holidays. Free.

New York. Hall of Fame for Great Americans, 1 Fifth Ave. Medals. Open to public 10–5 daily. Free.

New York. The Jewish Museum, 92nd St. and Fifth Ave. Coins, medals, tokens, numismatic literature. Some available to scholars only. Open to public 11–6 Monday through Thursday and Sunday. Closed national and Jewish holidays. Admission charged.

North Carolina

Charlotte. Mint Museum of Art, 501 Hempstead Place. Coins, paper money, other related items, equipment from the old Charlotte Mint. Open to scholars for study and to the public 10–5 Tuesday through Friday, 2–5 weekends, closed national holidays. Free.

Highlands. Money Museum. Coins, medals, tokens, paper money, numismatic literature. Open to public 9:30–6 daily in season. $2 admission.

Ohio

Columbus. Ohio Historical Center, 17th Ave. and I-71. Coins, medals, tokens, paper money. Some items in storage and available only to scholars. Open to public 9–5 Monday through Saturday, 1–5 Sunday and holidays, closed Christmas and New Year's Day. Free.

Fairborn. Air Force Museum, Wright-Patterson Air Force Base. Air Force insignia, decorations, medals. Open to public 9–5 weekdays, 10–6 weekends, closed Christmas. Free.

Marietta. Campus Maritus Museum. Coins, medals, paper money. Some items in storage available by appointment. Open to public 9–5 Monday through Saturday, 1–5 Sunday, closed Thanksgiving, Christmas, and New Year's Day. $1 admission for adults.

Milan. Milan Historical Museum, 10 Edison Dr. Coins, medals, tokens, paper money. Open to public 1–5 daily except Monday, closed Oct. 1 to April 1. Free.

Oxford. Miami University will have a display of Greek and Roman coins when its new museum opens.

Piqua. Johnson Farm, 9845 N. Hardin Rd. Indian peace medals. Open to public 10–5 Tuesday through Sunday, closed November through March. $1 for adults, $.50 for unaccompanied children 12 and under.

Wapakoneta. Neil Armstrong Museum. Medals. Open to public 9:30–5 Monday through Saturday, 1–5 Sunday and holidays, closed Christmas, Thanksgiving, New Year's Day. Admission $1.

Oklahoma

Oklahoma City. Oklahoma Science and Arts Foundation, 3000 Pershing Blvd. in Fair Park. Coins, medals, paper money available to scholars only. Museum open to public 9–5 Monday through Saturday, 1–5 Sunday, closed national holidays. Free.

Oregon

Biggs. Maryhill Museum of Fine Arts, on Highway 197. Awards and medals. Open daily 9–5:30 March 15–November 15.

Jacksonville. Jacksonville Museum. Coins, medals, tokens, paper money. Open to public 9–5 Monday through Saturday, 12–5 Sunday, June through August. Closed Mondays September through May, and Christmas, New Year's Day, and Thanksgiving. Free.

Pennsylvania

Drums. Kramer's Nesco Manor, Inc., Route 309. Large collection of wooden money. Open to public 1–9 daily. Free.

Franklin Center. The Franklin Mint Museum. Coins, large collection of medals, some tokens, and related items. Open to public 9–5 Monday through Saturday, 12–5 Sunday, closed Easter, Thanksgiving, Christmas, and New Year's Day. Free.

Pittsburgh. Carnegie Museum of Natural History, 4400 Forbes Ave. Large collection of coins, medals, tokens, paper money, and numismatic literature. Open to scholars only at present. Museum open 10–5 Tuesday through Sunday, closed legal holidays. Contributions accepted.

South Carolina

Camden. Blue Ridge Numismatic Association. Opened June 20, 1975. Paul E. Garland, director.

Columbia. South Carolina Confederate Relic Room and Museum, World War Memorial Building, Sumter St. at Pendleton. Coins, medals, tokens, paper money, numismatic literature. Open to public 9–5 Monday through Friday, closed national and state holidays. Free.

South Dakota

Pierre. South Dakota State Historical Museum, Memorial Building, Capitol Ave. Medals, tokens, paper money. Most open to scholars only. Museum open to the public 8–5 Monday through Friday, 10–5 Saturday, 1–5 Sunday, closed national holidays. Free.

Tennessee

Harrogate. Lincoln Room, Lincoln Memorial University. Coins, medals, tokens, paper money. Open to public 9–5 Monday through Friday, closed academic holidays. Free.

Memphis. The Memphis Academy of Arts Library, Overton Park. Medals. Open to public 8–5 Tuesday, Thursday, Friday, 8–10 Monday and Wednesday, 9–12 Saturday, closed national holidays. Free.

Memphis. Union Planters National Bank of Memphis Money Museum. Coins, medals, tokens, paper money, numismatic literature, other related items. Open to public 10–2 Monday through Friday, closed national holidays. Free.

197

Texas

Kingsville. Texas A & I University museum. Texas commemoratives, paper money, medals. Open to public 8 a.m.–12 p.m., 1 p.m.–5 p.m. Monday through Friday, 9 a.m.–12 p.m. Saturday, 2:30–5 Sunday.

Nacogdoches. Stone Fort Museum. Coins, paper money, numismatic literature. Open to public 9–5 Monday through Saturday, 1–5 Sunday, closed Christmas and New Year's Day. Free.

Virginia

Richmond. Virginia Museum, Boulevard and Grove Ave. Coins, medals. Open to public 11–5 Tuesday through Saturday, 1–5 Sunday, closed national holidays. Admission $.50.

Vermont

Bennington. Bennington Museum, Inc. Coins and paper money of Vermont. Open to public 9–6 daily in summer, 9:30–4:30 daily spring and fall. Closed Thanksgiving and December, January, and February. Admittance $1.50 for adults, $.50 for children under 18, children under 12 free.

Washington

Seattle. Seattle Art Museum, Volunteer Park. Coins, medals. Open to public 10–5 Tuesday through Sunday, also 7–10 p.m. Thursday, closed national holidays. Free.

Yakima. Yakima Valley Historical Museum. Coins, medals, paper money. Open to public 10–4 Wednesday through Friday, 2–5 Sunday. Closed for remodeling at present.

Wisconsin

Oconto. Oconto County Historical Society Museum, 917 Park Ave. Coins, medals, tokens, paper money, numismatic literature available to scholars only. Museum open 9–5 Monday through Saturday, 2–5 Sunday, closed national holidays. Free.

Reprinted by permission of Amos Press, Sidney, Ohio.

III

GLOSSARY OF
NUMISMATIC TERMS

ABOUT UNCIRCULATED Showing the merest trace of wear from any cause.

ADJUSTMENT (1) Filing down the face of an overweight planchet. Such filing marks often survive the coining process. This is most common to 18th century gold coins; (2) Arranging of a die in the press to attain correct striking. Coins struck during this adjustment process are abnormal in various ways and are known as adjustment trial pieces and are characteristically poorly struck.

ALLOY Mixture of more than one metal, usually preceded by the name of the most predominant or most important metal in the mix, such as nickel alloy.

ALTERED Deliberately changed, usually unofficially and usually with the intent of increasing numismatic value of the fraudulent piece.

ASSAY Analytic test or trial to ascertain the fineness, weight, or consistency of precious metals.

ATTRIBUTION The identification of a numismatic item by characteristics such as issuing authority, date, mint, denomination, and metal in which the item was struck.

AUCTION Method of selling by which items are presented for sale to the highest bidder.

AUTHENTICATION Authoritative determination of the genuineness of a numismatic item.

BAG MARKS Minor abrasions on an otherwise uncirculated coin, caused by contact between coins in a mint bag.

BANK NOTE A promissory note issued by a bank in useful denominations, payable to bearer and intended to circulate as money.

BILLON A low-grade alloy used for some minor coin issues consisting usually of a mixture of silver and copper, and sometimes coated with a silver wash.

BULLION Uncoined precious metal in the form of bars, plates, or ingots.

CABINET FRICTION Slight surface wear on a coin caused by friction between it and the tray or envelope in which it is contained.

200

CARTWHEELING Specular surfaces on coins as struck. Appears as a matte surface.

CHERRY A slang expression referring to a choice coin, unknown to the owner to be such.

CHERRY PICKING A slang expression for the act of selecting a choice coin from a dealer's stock when the owner is ignorant of its special desirability.

CLASHED DIES Obverse and reverse dies that have come together in the striking process without a planchet in place. Coins produced thereafter from such a pair of dies usually show mirror image traces of the die on the opposite side.

CLIPPED PLANCHET Planchet not fully round, due usually to slippage of the sheet causing planchet punch to overlap a previously punched hole or the edge of the strip.

COINING PROCESS The application of a device to a piece of metal by a coin-issuing authority whereby it becomes a coin. The process may be accomplished by casting, roller, rocker-die pressure, or high pressure impact. In modern times the process usually involves stamping the coin in a die cavity formed by two dies coming together against a piece of metal within a closely fitting collar die.

COMMEMORATIVE A piece issued to mark, honor, or observe an event, place, or person, or to preserve its memory.

CONDITION CENSUS Term introduced by Dr. William H. Sheldon to denote the finest specimen and average condition of next five finest known of a given variety of large cents. Today catalogers are utilizing the term with other series.

COUNTERFEIT An object made to imitate a genuine numismatic piece with intent to defraud and deceive, regardless of whether the intended fraud is primarily monetary or numismatic.

COUNTERMARK A punch mark officially applied to a coin or to a segment of the coin to change its value and/or to revalidate it where issued or elsewhere.

DATE The statement fixed to a numismatic item that specifies the date and sometimes the place of manufacture, if a mint mark is with it.

DEVICE The principal element, such as a portrait, shield, or heraldic emblem, of the design on the obverse and reverse of the coin.

DIE A hardened metal punch, the face of which carries intaglio or incuse mirror-image of the device to be impressed on one side of the planchet.

DIE PROOF An impression, usually on India or rice paper, of intaglio engraving. Not used in connection with a proof of an entire note but of an individual engraving, usually a portrait.

DIE STATE A stage of a die's life distinguished from other states by new cracks or by polishing or something else happening to it but not preventing its further use.

DIE VARIETY A coin having the same characteristics as all other pieces struck from a given die or given pair of dies. A different stage or state does not make a new variety.

ELECTROTYPE A copy or reproduction of a coin made by the electroplating process.

ERROR A coin evidencing a mistake made in its manufacture.

FACE The surface of a coin, referred to as either the obverse or the reverse.

FIAT MONEY The name formerly given to paper money that was issued by a government but which was not redeemable in coin or bullion.

FORGERY An unauthorized copy made with intent to deceive.

GEM A flawless piece.

GOBRECHT DOLLARS A series of twenty varieties of U.S. pattern coins struck in 1836, 1838, and 1839 and restruck at the Philadelphia Mint. Their dies were engraved by Christian Gobrecht, assistant engraver of the U.S. mint in Philadelphia, whose name appears on some varieties.

GREEN BACKS Legal tender, non-interest-bearing United States circulating notes first issued in 1862, their backs being printed in green ink.

HARD TIMES TOKEN An unofficial large cent size copper token struck in a wide variety from 1834–1841, serving as de facto currency, and bearing a politically inspired legend.

HOARD   Usually a deposit of coins, secreted at some time in the past, discovered accidentally.

HUB   Piece of steel with a design on it used to make working dies; will be either incuse or in relief opposite the working dies and the same as subsequent coins.

IMITATION   That which is made or produced as a copy, and usually not in violation of counterfeit laws.

IMPAIRED   Damaged or mishandled; an object that is in less than new condition through other than normal wear and tear in circulation.

IMPRINT   The name of the printer or engraver on paper money and other documents and forms.

INCUSE   Intaglio; the opposite of bas-relief; design is recessed rather than raised.

INTRINSIC   As applied to value, the net metallic value as distinguished from face value.

KNIFE EDGE   Same as wire edge.

LEGAL TENDER   Currency explicitly determined by a government to be acceptable in the discharge of debts.

LEGEND   The inscription on a numismatic item.

LETTERED EDGE   Intaglio lettering milled onto the edge of a coin before striking, or raised lettering on the edge of a coin produced by the use of a segmented collar die at the time of striking.

LOGO   (1) Multiple digit handpunch used to punch date digits into a hub or die; (2) emblem or trademark.

MAIL BID SALE   Auction by mail bids only.

MARK—MINTMASTER'S OR ASSAYER'S   Single or multiple initials, monogram, or symbol identifying the mintmaster or chief assayer responsible for the coin on which the mark appears.

MATTE PROOF   A proof coin with a finely granulated surface, officially produced by the issuing authority. Matte proofs were produced mostly around and just following the beginning of the 20th century.

MILLED COIN   By contrast with a hammered coin, a piece produced by pressure indirectly rather than directly applied, and the edge of which has been rolled or up-set.

MILLED EDGE   Prior to use of collar dies, the edge design was milled onto the edge of the planchet before the minting process. After the introduction of collar dies, milling of edges was introduced to thicken the outside border of a planchet so that the border ridge or design would be adequately raised when striking takes place.

MINT LUSTER   The sheen or bloom on the surface of an uncirculated numismatic object resulting from the centrifugal flow of metal caused by striking with dies. Mint luster or bloom is somewhat frosty in appearance as opposed to the mirror-like smoothness of the field of a proof.

MINT MARK   A letter or other symbol, sometimes of privy nature, indicating the mint of origin.

MINT PACKAGED SET   A set of coins packaged at the mint.

MINT SET   One coin of each denomination from a given mint in a given year.

MISSTRIKE   An error in striking.

NATIONAL BANK NOTE   Paper money issued in the United States by national banks from 1863 through 1929 and secured by government bonds or other collateral.

NATIONAL GOLD BANK NOTE   National Bank Notes payable in gold coin and issued by some California banks pursuant to authorization by Act of July 12, 1870.

NICKEL THREE CENTS   Three cent pieces of 75 percent copper and 25 percent nickel coined in the United States from 1865 to 1889 and distinguished from the silver three cent pieces.

NUMISMATIST   A person knowledgeable in numismatics.

OBVERSE   The side of a numismatic item that bears the principal design or legend, often as prescribed by the issuing authority.

OFFICIAL ISSUE   An authorized issue that has been given specific official sanction.

OVERDATE   A later date superimposed over a prior year's dated die.

OVERMINT MARK   Mark of one mint superimposed over the mark of a different mint.

OVERSTRIKE   A coin produced by use of a previously struck coin as a planchet, usually of a different design or different year.

PATINA   Natural coloring acquired by a coin with the passage of time; or as a result of oxidation produced by certain soils and moisture thereon. Patina may be artificially applied by a manufacturer using acids to bring out detail and develop an artistic finish.

PATTERN   A proposed coin, prepared officially by the mint or prepared unofficially by an outside entrepreneur usually for submission to a coin-issuing authority. A pattern may be struck in a variety of metals on a normal or thicker than normal planchet. Some patterns, particularly modern ones, are struck in considerable numbers for presentation or propaganda purposes or with a view to exploiting coin collectors.

PLANCHET   The disc of metal or other material on which the dies of the coin are impressed; also called blanc, disc, and flan.

PRESENTATION   The act of offering a numismatic item to some person on special occasion or event such as the inauguration of a coinage. The object so bestowed is sometimes referred to as a presentation piece.

PROOF   A piece produced by a technique involving specially prepared dies and planchets and usually special striking, resulting in particular sharpness of detail and a virtually flawless surface, usually mirror-like or matte surface over the field at least, sometimes with a frosted design.

PROOF-LIKE   Having surfaces as flawless and brilliant, or nearly so, as a proof but struck from working dies and sold to collectors as above-average specimens. The term originated with and is generally applied to Canadian uncirculated mint-produced and mint-packaged sets.

PROOF SET   A set of one proof coin of each current denomination issued by a recognized mint for a specific year.

RARE   A comparative term denoting a high degree of scarcity.

REEDED EDGE   The result of a minting process that creates vertical serrations on the edge of a coin. This process is performed by a collar die simultaneously with the striking of the faces of the coin.

REPLICA   A copy of the original, a facsimile.

RESTRIKE   A numismatic item produced from original dies at a later date; in the case of a coin, usually not with the intention of meeting monetary requirements.

SCRIP   Paper currency usually of denominations less than one dollar issued as a substitute for currency to private persons.

SILVER THREE CENTS   Smallest U.S. silver coin, issued from 1851 through 1873 in three main varieties, and two weights and metallic composition.

SLEEPER   A numismatic item, the rarity or future value of which is not generally recognized.

SLIDER   A coin actually below the grade indicated but very close to it; such as an almost uncirculated coin offered as uncirculated.

SLUG   A term applied to the $50 gold coin issued by various private mints in California from 1851 to 1855 occurring in both round and octagonal shapes.

SPECIMEN   A synonym for a numismatic item, e.g., a very rare specimen.

TRIAL PIECE   A piece struck at any stage in the preparation of regular dies up to the point of their being put to use for the striking of actual coins.

TRIME   Silver 3 cent piece.

TYPE   Main design for a series, regardless of modification at any time.

TYPE SET   Collection comprised of one coin of each desired series.

UNCIRCULATED   A piece in new condition as issued by the mint. If a given coin has evidence of handling, it is no longer uncirculated.

UNIQUE   Extant in only one known specimen.

VARIETY   Difference between the product of two different dies from the same hub, or between products of the working dies from two different hubs.

WEIGHT   U.S. coins are officially weighed in Troy measure, by grains, with 480 grains to the ounce. (Avoirdupois ounce is 437.5 grains.)

WHIZZING   Any process, such as buffing, burnishing, polishing, acid treatment, and/or wire brushing, by which any metal is moved or removed on the surface of a coin to make it look better than it actually is.

WIRE EDGE   Slight flange on coins caused by heavy striking pressure, often characteristic on proof coins. The metal is squeezed up the side of the face dies by the collar die.

WORKING DIE   Die used to strike coins directly as distinguished from a master die or developmental hubs.

WORKING HUB   The transfer die with a relief design (usually) from which working dies are made.

Reprinted from "The Dictionary of Numismatic Terms." American Numismatic Association, Colorado Springs, Co.

BIBLIOGRAPHY

> When you steal from one author, it's plagiarism; if you
> steal from many, it's research.
>
> Wilson Mizner, 1907

*M*uch of the information within this book comes from investment counselors and professional numismatists who possess a great deal more knowledge in their respective fields than I do. However, this book was written to act as a guide for rare coin investment, drawing upon expertise from many related fields and condensing that expertise into a more useable form.

Akers, David W., *United States Gold Coins Volume III*, Englewood, Ohio: Paramount Publications, 1976.

American Numismatic Association, *For Collectors of Coins, Paper Money, Tokens and Medals*, Colorado Springs, Co.: American Numismatic Association, 1979.

————, *The Dictionary of Numismatic Terms*, Colorado Springs, Co.: American Numismatic Association, 1975.

Bailey, M., "The New Gold Rush," *Barron's*, March 5, 1979.

Bartlett, John, *Familiar Quotations: A Collection of Passages, Phrases, and Proverbs Traced to Their Sources in Ancient and Modern Literature.* Edited by Emily Morison Beck. 14th ed. revised and enlarged. Boston: Little, Brown & Co., 1968.

Bowers, Q.D., *High Profits from Rare Coin Investing*, Los Angeles, CA.: Bowers & Ruddy Galleries, Inc., 1974.

————, *Adventures with Rare Coins*, Los Angeles, CA.: Bowers & Ruddy Galleries, Inc., 1979.

————, *The History of United States Coinage*, Los Angeles, CA.: Bowers & Ruddy Galleries, 1979.

Bressett, K., and Kosoff, A., *Official A.N.A. Grading Standards for U.S. Coins*, Western Publishing Co., Racine, Wisconsin: American Numismatic Association, 1977.

Button, S., "How States Stack Up," *Money Magazine*, February 1979.

Cline, J.H., *Standing Liberty Quarters*, 1976.

Coin World, *Coin World Almanac*, Sidney, Ohio: Amos Press, Inc., 1975.

Commodity Research Bureau, Inc., *Commodity Yearbook*, Commodity Research Bureau, 1955.

———, 1966.

———, 1978.

Council of Economic Advisors, *Economic Indicators*, Washington, D.C.: United States Government Printing Office, January 1978.

———, December 1978.

Dauten, C.A., and Valentine, L.M., *Business Cycles and Forecasting*, Chicago, Ill.: South-Western Publishing Company, 1978.

deMarinis, Joseph, *The Rare Coin Market: Explaining Rare Coin Price Cycles*, New York, N.Y.: Sinclair & deMarinis & Co., February 1981.

Devine, J., *Detecting Counterfeit Coins*, Newbury Park, Calif.: Heigh-Ho Printing Corp., 1975.

———, *Detecting Counterfeit Gold Coins*, Newbury Park, Calif.: Heigh-Ho Printing Corp., 1977.

Doty, Richard G., *Money of the World*, New York: Grosset & Dunlap, 1978.

Dow Jones & Company, "Ways to Buy Gold," *The Wall Street Journal*, March 8, 1979.

———, "Speculators Unsettle U.S. Rare-Coin Market," *The Wall Street Journal*, March 2, 1981.

Economic Statistics Bureau of Washington D.C., *The Handbook of Economic Statistics*, Washington, D.C.: Economic Statistics Bureau, August-September, 1978.

Ehrbar, A.F., "Looking Back on a Decade of Misery," *Fortune*, February 1976.

Hall, David, and David Hunt, "31 Year Price History of High Quality U.S. Rare Coins," *Inside View*, 1980. Newport Beach, California.

———, "Go for the Big Score," *Inside View*, June 1981. Newport Beach, Ca.

Hancock, Virgil, and Spanbauer, Larry, *Standard Catalog of United States Altered and Counterfeit Coins*, New York: Sanford J. Durst, 1979.

Hardy, C.C., and Crowell, T.Y., *Dun & Bradstreet's Guide to Your Investments*, New York: Thomas Y. Cromwell Publishers, 1979.

Harriman, A., ed., *The Coin Dealer Newsletter,* Monthly Summary February 1979.

———, January 5, 1979.

———, March 16, 1979.

———, March 7, 1980.

———, June 26, 1981.

———, July 24, 1981.

———, December 11, 1981.

———, January 8, 1982.

Haskett, J.A., "How Do Bankers Invest Their Money?," *Burroughs Clearing House,* June 1974.

Kiplinger, Austin H., and Barach, Arnold B., *The Exciting 80's,* Washington, D.C.: The Kiplinger Washington Editors, Inc., 1979.

Knauth, Percy A., "Coins Go Up as Fabled Collection Is Sold at Auction," *Smithsonian,* March 1980.

Liebler, M., "Alternative Investments for the Sophisticated Investor," *Commodities,* January 1978.

Lindman, C.J., "Rare Coins in Your KEOGH," *Barron's,* March 12, 1979.

Littleton Rare Coin Investment Company, *Invest in U.S. Rare Coins,* 1978.

Miller, Wayne, *An Analysis of Morgan and Peace Dollars,* Helena, Montana: Wayne Miller, 1976.

Numismatic Investments of Florida, *Rare Coin Investment,* 1978. Miami, Fl.

Owen, J.D., "Workweeks and Leisure: An Analysis of Trends, 1948–1975," *Monthly Labor Review,* Washington, D.C.: U.S. Bureau of Labor Statistics, August 1976.

Parsons, J.D., *Color and Toning on Uncirculated and Proof Coins,* Rare Coin Review, No 34.

Perschke, Walter, *The Numisco Letter,* Chicago, Ill.: International Financial Publishers, June 30, 1980.

———, June 25, 1981.

Porter, Thomas W., and Alkire, Durwood L., *Wealth: How to Achieve It!,* Reston, Virginia: Reston Publishing Co., 1976.

Raymond, Wayte, *The Standard Catalogue of United States Coins,* Raymond Wayte, Inc. NY.

Reed, M., *Cowles Complete Encyclopedia of U.S. Coins,* New York: Cowles Book Company, 1969.

Ronalds, Nicholas, "While Money in Your Pocket Loses Value, Rare Old Coins Are Appreciating Smartly," *The Wall Street Journal,* August 27, 1979.

Ruddy, J., *Photograde.* Los Angeles, CA: Bowers & Ruddy Galleries.

Salomon Brothers, "Bonds and Foreign Exchange May Be the Only Bargains Left," *Investment Policy,* New York, June 15, 1981.

Seeger, M., "Gold: Many Seek to Share in Glow," *Los Angeles Times,* February 18, 1979.

Stack, H.G., "Coins as an Estate Asset," *Trusts and Estates,* January, 1976.

Taxay, Don, *The Comprehensive Catalogue and Encyclopedia of United States Coins,* New York: Scott Publishers, 1970.

U.S. News and World Report, Inc., "New Gold Rush Sends Prices Soaring," *U.S. News and World Report,* February 19, 1979.

_____, "It's Never Too Early to Plan," February 26, 1979.

_____, "Runaway Inflation," March 12, 1979.

_____, "Carter's Strategy," March 19, 1979.

_____, "Social Security," June 1, 1981.

_____, "Reagan's Tax Program," June 22, 1981.

Westerman, S., ed., *CBS News 1978 Almanac,* Hammond Almanac, 1977.

Wohlers, A.H., & Company, *Collection Insurance,* Chicago, Illinois: Wohlers Insurance Company, 1979.

Yeoman, R.S., *A Guide Book of United States Coins,* 16th ed., Western Publishing Inc., Racine, Wisconsin, 1963.

_____, 17th ed., 1964.

_____, 18th ed., 1965.

_____, 21st ed., 1968.

_____, 23rd ed., 1970.

_____, 27th ed., 1974.

_____, 28th ed., 1975.

_____, 32nd ed., 1979.

_____, 33rd ed., 1980.

_____, 34th ed., 1981.

_____, 35th ed., 1982.

INDEX